# The Comprehensive Autism Planning System (CAPS) for Individuals with Asperger Syndrome, Autism, and Related Disabilities

## Integrating Best Practices Throughout the Student's Day

Shawn A. Henry

Brenda Smith Myles

Foreword by Ruth Aspy and Barry Grossman

© 2007 Autism Asperger Publishing Co.
P.O. Box 23173
Shawnee Mission, Kansas 66283-0173
www.asperger.net ▪ 913.897.1004

Publisher's Cataloging-in-Publication

Henry, Shawn A.

The comprehensive autism planning system (CAPS) for individuals with Asperger syndrome, autism, and related disabilities : integrating best practices throughout the student's day / Shawn A. Henry, Brenda Smith Myles. -- 1st ed. -- Shawnee Mission, Kan. : Autism Asperger Pub. Co., 2007.

p. ; cm.

ISBN-13: 978-1-934575-03-1
ISBN-10: 1-934575-03-8
LCCN: 2007929036
Includes bibliographical references and index.

1. Autistic children--Education. 2. Autistic youth--Education. 3. Asperger's syndrome--Patients--Education. 4. Autism in children. 5. Asperger's syndrome in children. 6. Learning disabled children--Education. 7. Teachers of children with disabilities--Handbooks, manuals, etc. I. Myles, Brenda Smith. II. Title.

LC4717 .H46 2007          2007929036
371.94--dc22              0706

This book is designed in Lucida Sans and American Typewriter.

Printed in the United States of America.

# Dedication

*This book would not be a reality without all of the support and encouragement of family and friends.*

*To my parents for instilling in me dedication to work and service to community.*

*To my wife, Sally, and children, Will, Aaron, and Hayden, who have blessed me with their unconditional love, inspiration, and energy.*

*To my co-author and friend for her tireless work and energy to make this book a reality.*

*To all the family members of individuals with autism who have shared their story, which in turn has shaped mine.*

*– Shawn Henry*

# Acknowledgments

We would like to thank the many individuals who contributed to this project: Andi Babkie, Teresa Cardon, Christina Carnahan, Amy Bixler Coffin, Yu-Chi Chou, Joyce Downing, Jill Hudson, Hyo Jung Lee, Sherry Moyer, Kai-Chien Tien, and Sheila Smith, who wrote book chapters and case studies; Kirsten McBride, Vivian Strand, Ginny Biddulph, and Megan Duncan, who turned words into a book; Rhonda Bowen, Laura Bullard, Marita Burrow, Lezli Carson, Karla Dennis, Katie Lents, Jennifer Stanley, and Lisa Toler, whose visual supports appear in the book; Judy Halvorson and Jason's dad, who allowed the CAPS they had developed to be used as case studies; and the students who used the CAPS model at school and at home.

# Foreword

It was an honor to be invited to write the Foreword for *The Comprehensive Autism Planning System (CAPS) for Individuals with Asperger Syndrome, Autism, and Related Disabilities*. We became familiar with the CAPS through the "matchmaking" of the visionary Brenda Smith Myles. We always put great stock in what Brenda says. She told us that she has seen three recent advances in the field that have the potential to significantly impact individuals with ASD. The CAPS is one of them. Brenda knew about our work – the Ziggurat Model (we were humbled when she identified the Ziggurat as one of the three advances). Knowing the CAPS, she was able to see that, while either model is effective alone, the effectiveness of each would be strengthened when used in combination. As a result, Brenda arranged a meeting between Shawn Henry, the creator of the CAPS, and ourselves, and we were immediately impressed by the elegance of CAPS. Brenda was right.

CAPS is a reflection of its creator. In his role as a state and national leader, Shawn serves as an advocate for individuals with ASD. The CAPS model illustrates his ability to make significant change through realistic and practical means. The CAPS is simple, yet powerful.

Best practice is defined as "a superior method or innovative practice that contributes to the improved performance of an organization" (Visitask, n.d.).[1] Shawn Henry and Brenda Smith

[1]Visitask. (n.d.). *Best practice.* Retrieved June 2, 2007, from http://www.visitask.com/best-practice-g.asp

Myles present a true best practice – the CAPS. The CAPS helps staff to optimize a student's daily program in a way that incorporates needed supports. It is a critical piece that has been missing for too long. Thanks to CAPS, parents and team members will have the how, what, when, and where of intervention spelled out in a clear and meaningful way. Those who work with students with ASD will find CAPS to be an indispensable tool.

Shawn and Brenda clearly describe each element of the CAPS model in a well-organized text. Throughout the book, the authors and expert contributors highlight a variety of evidence-based strategies that correspond to each area of the CAPS. The authors also clearly outline the actual process of completing a CAPS as a multidisciplinary team. Finally, case studies help to illustrate the flexibility of the CAPS model and its use for individuals with a range of needs across age groups, educational levels, and settings.

Planning a comprehensive intervention is only the first step. All too often, very detailed IEP plans seem to go nowhere. Without faithful implementation, even an excellent intervention plan is worthless. CAPS is "where the rubber hits the road." Through the CAPS book, Shawn and Brenda provide an invaluable tool that ensures that goals translate into intervention.

> – Ruth Aspy and Barry Grossman, authors of
> *The Ziggurat Model: A Framework for Designing*
> *Comprehensive Interventions for Individuals with*
> *High-Functioning Autism and Asperger Syndrome*

# Table of Contents

ix

# Beginning with the End in Mind

**A**s multidisciplinary teams, including parents, strive to develop meaningful educational opportunities for individuals with autism spectrum disorders (ASD), they would do well to begin with the end in mind. That is, the ultimate goal of a team is to create a comprehensive daily schedule for the student that embeds the supports the student needs to be successful. In addition, the daily schedule should include the continual development of skills and measurement of those skills with a vision of how this will affect the student now and in the future. This is achieved through well-organized lesson plans with clearly defined objectives and goals. When working with students with ASD, the team must pay special attention to addressing students' social, communication, and sensory needs. This is exactly where the Comprehensive Autism Planning System (CAPS) comes in.

## Assets of CAPS

The CAPS system was developed for several reasons. First and foremost it was created to ensure that students' needs are being met

1

across the academic day. In addition, it is founded on the recognition that students with ASD have complex needs in multiple areas, including structure/modifications, reinforcement, sensory, and communication/social skills.

| | | | | Comprehensive Autism Planning System (CAPS) | | | | |
|---|---|---|---|---|---|---|---|---|
| Child/Student: _____ | | | | | | | | *ss=state standard |
| Time | Activity | Targeted Skills to Teach | Structure/ Modifications | Reinforcement | Sensory Strategies | Communication/ Social Skills | Data Collection | Generalization Plan |
| | | | | | | | | |
| | | | | | | | | |
| | | | | | | | | |
| | | | | | | | | |
| | | | | | | | | |
| | | | | | | | | |

Further, the CAPS system is individualized. Each student has his or her own CAPS, planned by a multidisciplinary team that understands the student's unique needs. And it is comprehensive. CAPS's structure takes into account all the activities in which the student participates and ensures that supports are integrated throughout the day in a smooth, systematic manner. Finally, CAPS is universal. That is, it can be used with students from preschool to college age and with students whose skills may be described as functional or as gifted. Further, it can be used at home, at school, or in the community. Thus, CAPS's structured flexibility encourages the use of supports and methodologies that match the student's needs. In fact, CAPS permits a variety of methodologies or just one methodology to be present throughout the child's day.

CAPS was originally used to address student transition as illustrated in the following.

Sally's team worked with her extensively during fifth grade to ensure that she was successful. A variety of supports were put in place during her day, which resulted in increased time spent in general education, decreased meltdowns, and a Circle of Friends who joined her at lunch, recess, and field trips. Sally appeared happy, as did her parents and the rest of her multidisciplinary team. When Sally moved to sixth grade, her resource room teacher met with the sixth-grade multidisciplinary team (of which no one had been on Sally's previous team) to describe the supports that helped her be successful the previous year.

The team felt well prepared. However, Sally's early days in sixth grade did not go well. It appeared that Sally did not know how to use the supports that were put in place, and Sally's behavior revealed that she was anxious and unhappy. The team was puzzled. Soon they called the resource room teacher and explained the challenges they and Sally were experiencing. The resource room teacher, Mr. Henry, often accused of being a pack-rat, prepared for the meeting by going through all his old files and subsequently writing out Sally's fifth-grade daily schedule and organizing the photographs of all of Sally's supports that he had taken the previous year. The resource room teacher then met with the new team and presented Sally's fifth-grade schedule activity by activity, including photographs of the supports and structures that were in place throughout the day. Once the sixth-grade multidisciplinary team saw this structure, they realized the complexity of Sally's needs, and understood better what supports she needed. At the team's request, Mr. Henry walked them through Sally's day, identifying supports and structures needed. Thus, CAPS was created.

CAPS can facilitate the transition of students from one grade to the next, as illustrated in more detail in one of the case studies in Chapter 11. A clearly developed plan with pictures of the supports used throughout the student's day can help a receiving team develop a plan for the upcoming year. A notation on the CAPS that a student needs a visual support, outlining each activity and accompanying pictures of the support, helps the new team create a structure that is meaningful and consistent for the student. In addition, educator time is saved. That is, the educator has a digital picture or other visual image of the support or modification used by the child, so development is often just a matter of replication or adaptation.

# Professional Development

In addition to supporting student success in school, CAPS also fosters targeted professional development. Because CAPS identifies supports for each of the student's daily activities, it is possible for educational professionals working with the student to readily identify the methods, supports, and structures in which they, the adults, need training. For example, if a student's schedule indicates that priming is needed prior to math class, it is essential that the math teacher understand the concept of priming and how to implement it. This educator's professional development plan, then, structured directly from the CAPS, will include training on priming. By its very focus, CAPS facilitates professional development. Team members working together to develop the student's CAPS who have expertise in a given area become the instructors who describe, model, and support adult application of new skills.

# Addressing Current Mandates and Educational Trends

Far-reaching changes were proposed in the often controversial No Child Left Behind Act (NCLB; 2001), whose basic purpose is to increase study achievement. The guiding principles behind NCLB are accountability and scientifically based instruction provided by highly qualified and effective teachers (U.S. Department of Education, 2002). CAPS is compatible with each of these requirements.

*Accountability* occurs through measures of student skills through a mechanism known as adequate yearly progress (AYP), wherein states establish standards and measure student achievement toward these standards (Yell, Drasgow, & Lowrey, 2005). Built into CAPS are targeted skills to teach as well as data collection. Skills include individualized education program (IEP) goals as well as state standards. As a result, data are collected throughout the student's day in all settings.

*Scientifically based instruction* is also inherent in CAPS. Instruction embedded with the necessary supports to ensure student progress is provided throughout the day (Yell et al., 2005). That is, each activity is seen as a learning opportunity that occurs by implementation of evidence-based practices. Philosophically, CAPS charges that this instruction be provided in the student's least restrictive environment, preferably the general education setting whenever possible.

Compatible with NCLB is the response-to-intervention (RTI) movement founded upon data-based decision making and problem

CAPS ...

- ensures the student's needs are met throughout the school day
- recognizes the complex needs of students with ASD
- is individualized
- is comprehensive
- is systematic, yet flexible
- facilitates transition from one grade to the next
- facilitates professional development
- is compatible with current educational mandates and trends, including NCLB, RTI, and SWPBS

solving, evidence-based interventions, student performance, and continuous progress monitoring (Sugai & Horner, 2007). A ground-breaking document issued as a collaborative effort among 14 national organizations (ASHA, CASE, CEC et al., 2006) documents the following conditions and activities of RTI, each of which is addressed in CAPS:

- High-quality instructional and behavioral supports are provided throughout the day.

- Research-based intervention is implemented by qualified personnel.

- Student progress is continuously monitored using meaningful data.

- Decisions are made by a collaborative team of school staff who review student progress.

- Interventions address the individual student's difficulties at the needed level of intensity.

- A written document describing the specific components and structure of the process is used.

- Parent notification and involvement are documented.

CAPS also meets the guidelines established by statewide positive behavior supports (SWPBS), whose goals are to support (a) student social competence and academic achievement, (b) student behavior, (c) staff behavior, and (d) decision making. Through its goal-directed and individualized structure, CAPS designs a comprehensive program that meets the rigor of SWPBS (Sugai & Horner, 2007).

# Who Will Use the Comprehensive Autism Planning System (CAPS)?

This book is intended for anyone who has a vested interest in building the best possible educational program for the individual with ASD. The CAPS process is designed to be used by an educational team consisting of parents, general educators, special educators, paraprofessionals, speech-language pathologists, occupational therapists, physical therapists, administrators, psychologists, consultants, siblings, and others who are stakeholders in the student's education.

# Overview of the Book

This book introduces CAPS – a method of planning a student's daily schedule that ensures that all supports are in place to facilitate academic, social, and behavioral success. The book begins with an overview of CAPS, with succeeding chapters describing the supports that are integrated into CAPS. Separate chapters are not devoted to the first three columns of the CAPS (Time, Activity, Targeted Skills to Teach) because:

1. The first two are self-explanatory.

2. Targeted Skills to Teach include IEP goals and objectives as well as state standards or other measurable targets identified by the student's multidisciplinary team.

The book concludes with case studies that describe the application of the system with a preschool, elementary, and middle/high school student, as well as an example of home use.

## Summary

CAPS is a unique method of developing and implementing a meaningful program for a student with ASD. Its structure fosters consistent use of supports to ensure student success as well as data collection to measure that success. Compatible with current trends in education, including NCLB, RTI, and SWPBS, CAPS is simple and easy to use.

# References

ASHA, CASE, CEC, CLD, DLD, IDA, IRA, LDA, NASDSE, NASP, NCLD, NASP, NEA, ASSWAA. (2006, November). *New roles in response to interventions: Creating success in schools*. Washington, DC: Author.

Sugai, G., & Horner, R. (2007, March). *Statewide positive behavior supports and response to instruction: Lessons being learned*. Presentation at 4th Annual Conference on Positive Behavior Supports, Boston, MA.

U.S. Department of Education. (2002). *No Child Left Behind: A desktop reference*. Washington, DC: Education Publications Center.

Yell, M. L., Drasgow, E., & Lowrey, K. A. (2005). No Child Left Behind and students with autism spectrum disorders. *Focus on Autism and Other Developmental Disabilities, 20*, 130-139.

# The Comprehensive Autism Planning System

## CHAPTER 1

Multidisciplinary teams, including parents, spend a significant amount of time on a student's individualized education program (IEP), identifying present levels of performance as well as goals and objectives that will help the student be successful in school. Even though student outcomes are delineated in the IEP, it is often difficult to fully transfer them to a student's daily program (Aspy & Grossman, 2007).

For example, a student's IEP may indicate that she needs sensory input; yet educators, in particular general educators, often do not know what type of support should be provided and when it should occur. The same child may also need a choice board or a visual schedule to enhance performance. Such accommodations may not be listed on the IEP even though they are integral to the child's success, leading to frustration both for the teacher and the child, limitations in access to the general education curriculum, or severe behavior challenges.

# Using the Comprehensive Autism Planning System

The Comprehensive Autism Planning System (CAPS) is designed to provide an overview of a student's daily schedule by time and activity as well as the supports that she needs during each period. Following the development of the student's IEP, all educational professionals who work with the student develop the CAPS. Thus, the CAPS allows professionals and parents to answer the all-important question for students with an autism spectrum disorder (ASD): What supports does the student need for each activity?

As shown in Figure 1.1 (and the Appendix), the CAPS consists of a list of a student's daily tasks and activities, the times they occur, along with a thorough delineation of the supports needed to support student success. In addition, it includes space for making notations about data collection and how skills are to be generalized to other settings.

The CAPS consists of the following components developed from evidence-based best practices for students with ASD:

1. *Time.* This section indicates the clock time when each activity that the student engages in throughout the day takes place.

2. *Activity.* Activities include all tasks and activities throughout the day in which the student requires support. Academic periods (e.g., reading, math), nonacademic times (e.g., recess, lunch), and transitions between classes would all be considered activities.

3. *Targeted Skills to Teach.* This may include IEP goals, state standards, and/or general skills that lead to school success. These skills can serve as the basis for measuring response to intervention (RTI) or annual yearly progress (AYP).

**Figure 1.1. CAPS.**

## Comprehensive Autism Planning System (CAPS)

Child/Student: _____

*ss=state standard

| Time | Activity | Targeted Skills to Teach | Structure/ Modifications | Reinforcement | Sensory Strategies | Communication/ Social Skills | Data Collection | Generalization Plan |
|------|----------|--------------------------|--------------------------|---------------|--------------------|------------------------------|-----------------|---------------------|
|      |          |                          |                          |               |                    |                              |                 |                     |
|      |          |                          |                          |               |                    |                              |                 |                     |
|      |          |                          |                          |               |                    |                              |                 |                     |
|      |          |                          |                          |               |                    |                              |                 |                     |
|      |          |                          |                          |               |                    |                              |                 |                     |

*Note.* The owner of this book may download a copy of the CAPS form (either Word or pdf format) from www.asperger.net/CAPS User name: aapc; password: CAPS

The Comprehensive
Autism Planning System

4. *Structure/Modifications.* This can encompass a wide variety of supports, including placement in the classroom, visual supports (e.g., choice boards, visual schedules), peer supports (e.g., Circle of Friends, peer buddies), and instructional strategies (e.g., priming, self-monitoring).

5. *Reinforcement.* Student access to specific types of reinforcement as well as reinforcement schedules is listed under the reinforcement section of the CAPS.

6. *Sensory Strategies.* Sensory supports and strategies identified by an occupational therapist are listed in this CAPS area.

7. *Communication/Social Skills.* Specific communication goals or activities as well as supports are delineated here. Goals or activities may include (a) requesting help, (b) taking turns in conversation, or (c) protesting appropriately. Supports, which are also diverse, may encompass (a) language boards; (b) PECS (Picture Exchange Communication System; Frost & Bondy, 2002); or (c) other augmentative communication systems.

8. *Data Collection.* Data collection includes gathering information on behavior(s) to be documented during a specific activity. Typically, this section relates directly to IEP goals and objectives, behavioral issues, and state standards.

9. *Generalization Plan.* Because individuals with ASD often have problems generalizing information across settings, this section of the CAPS was developed to ensure that generalization of skills is built into the child's program.

The CAPS model may be used alone or in combination with another model – the Ziggurat Model (Aspy & Grossman, 2007). Each of these models is strong, but together they are even stronger.

The Ziggurat Model is designed to address true needs or underlying deficits that result in social, emotional, and behavioral concerns. The Intervention Ziggurat is the centerpiece of the Ziggurat Model.

**Ziggurat**

| Skills to Teach |
| Task Demands |
| Structure and Visual/Tactile |
| Reinforcement |
| Sensory Differences and Biological Needs |

It contains five levels in a hierarchical structure. Starting with the foundation level – Sensory Differences and Biological Needs – each level represents an area that must be addressed in order for an intervention plan to be comprehensive. Further, each level contributes to the effectiveness of the other levels. Underlying needs and characteristics related to ASD must be addressed – this is a key premise of the Ziggurat Model. To that end, the Ziggurat Model includes

**Individual Strengths and Skills Inventory (ISSI)**
Ruth Aspy, Ph.D., and Barry G. Grossman, Ph.D.

In designing effective intervention plans, it is important to be aware of individual strengths. Please describe strengths in the following areas:

Social

Behavior, Interests, and Activities

Communication

Sensory and Biological

Cognitive

Motor

Emotional

Aspy, R., & Grossman, B. (2007) *The Ziggurat model: A framework for designing comprehensive interventions for individuals with high-functioning autism and Asperger Syndrome.* Shawnee Mission, KS: Autism Asperger Publishing Company. www.asperger.net. Contact Ruth Aspy (aspy@texasautism.com) and Barry Grossman (grossman@texasautism.com) or visit www.texasautismcom

the Underlying Characteristics Checklist (UCC-HF or CL), which provides a snapshot of how ASD is expressed for an individual, and the Individual Strengths and Skills Inventory (ISSI).

To use the Ziggurat and CAPS together, the process begins with the completion of the UCC and ISSI to identify the child's autism and his strengths and skills. Then interventions are identified in each of the five Ziggurat levels, starting with Sensory Differences and Biological Needs, so that all the UCC and ISSI items are addressed. This information is then incorporated into the CAPS to ensure that the student's needs and interventions are addressed throughout the child's daily schedule with data collection and generalization built in.

# Ginny's CAPS

The following brief case study shows how CAPS was implemented for an 8-year-old student with ASD, Ginny. Ginny is in the second grade and tested in the "below-average" range on a test of cognitive ability. Ginny uses PECS (Frost & Bondy, 2002) to communicate, but shows limited generalization to school staff and none among peers. She receives her education in a kindergarten/first-grade resource room and is included during "specials" and early-morning calendar group.

Ginny has been demonstrating some behavioral issues related to transitions, attention to task, and interacting appropriately with peers. Observations in Ginny's classrooms confirmed behavioral issues identified as problematic and revealed an inconsistent use of supports. Ginny's team met to create a CAPS to match Ginny's daily schedule. A partial view of the CAPS is presented in Figure 1.2.

Similar to most students, Ginny's day begins before her first academic class. She starts with breakfast at school. As shown on the CAPS, Ginny will be learning three skills during this time: (a) making choices, (b) using a language board, and (c) following a schedule. Use of choice and language boards and the reinforcement is natural – eating the food she chooses from the breakfast menu.

While Ginny does not need sensory supports for this activity, she does require communication and social interventions. She has social questions on her language board and a visual support that illustrates table manners. Data collected include (a) frequency of making choices and (b) the number of times she used her language board.

## Figure 1.2. Ginny's CAPS.

## Comprehensive Autism Planning System (CAPS)

Child/Student: _____ Ginny _____

*ss=state standard

| Time | Activity | Targeted Skills to Teach | Structure/ Modifications | Reinforcement | Sensory Strategies | Communication/ Social Skills | Data Collection | Generalization Plan |
|------|----------|--------------------------|--------------------------|---------------|--------------------|-------------------------------|-----------------|---------------------|
| 7:30-7:55 | Breakfast | Choose breakfast using breakfast board<br><br>Using interactive language board<br><br>Independent schedule use | Choice board of breakfast items<br><br>Interactive language board<br><br>Visual schedule | Choice of food items | Not at this time | Have additional social language on board (i.e., greetings, questions)<br><br>Work on table manners | Data sheet for choice<br><br>Data on use of language board | Use language board during lunch or dinner at home |
| 8:05-8:20 | Independent morning work<br><br>Lunch count prep | Independent work of mastered math problems<br><br>Self-monitoring<br><br>Review menu for lunch choices<br><br>Charting lunch count<br><br>Collect and organize data (ss)<br><br>Follow two- and three-step oral directions (ss) | Visuals to break down task (1-5, raise hand, finished)<br><br>Visual focusing aid<br><br>Visual schedule<br><br>Priming for lunch count<br><br>Trained peer buddy | Complete 5 problems – get a break of her choice<br><br>Social reinforcement from peers | Ginny needs black construction paper box around problem to write in box<br><br>Slant board with textured paper underneath for more feedback<br><br>Sticky string for lunch graphing sheet | Follow general education classroom rules<br><br>Review lunch choices<br><br>Ginny will ask peers if they have one of the lunch choices by holding the choice up and saying the name (i.e., hamburger, sack lunch)<br><br>Interpersonal skills (proximity to peer) | Use of self-monitoring sheets, % independent<br><br>Data sheet for transitions | Self-monitoring in other subjects<br><br>Using peers' names throughout the school day |

| Time | Activity | Objectives | Instructional Strategies | Social | Sensory | Communication | Data | Generalization |
|---|---|---|---|---|---|---|---|---|
| 8:20–9:00 | 1) Attendance<br>2) Lunch count<br>3) Morning work<br>4) Calendar | Collect and organize data (ss)<br>Names of classmates<br>Reciprocal interaction with peers<br>Self-monitoring<br>Using language board for calendar skills<br>Measure calendar time (ss)<br>List days and months in order (ss) | Systematic prompting (least-most) for use of language board<br>Task analysis of morning work using pictures (she will put in finished slot when completed)<br>Visual schedule | Social reinforcement from peers | Sensory items available (lotion, koosh ball)<br>Change positions if lying on desk<br>Slant board | PECS book<br>Language board for lunch count<br>Language board for calendar activities<br>Interpersonal skills (proximity to peer) | Copy attendance from board<br>Language board use (+ if she uses board, * if she uses board and verbalizes)<br>Data sheet for transitions | Using classmates' names in hall, playground, lunch, etc. |
| 9:00–9:30 | SPECIALS<br>M Computer<br>T Library<br>W<br>TH Video | Using language board – increase MLU<br>Follow two- and three-step oral directions (ss)<br>Independent use of schedule for transitions | Trained peer buddies<br>Modified rules to game to increase communication<br>Visual schedule<br>Mini-schedule (task analysis) | Game playing<br>Movement<br>Social reinforcement from peers | Smaller and controlled setting | Reciprocal interaction with peers<br>Increasing MLU through use of language board<br>Turn taking<br>Cooperative learning groups | Data sheet for transitions<br>Data on use of language board | Use language boards during lunch and dinner at home |
| 9:35–10:00 | Whole-group<br>Reading<br>Spelling<br>Writing | Print legibly (ss)<br>Use active listening strategies (ss)<br>Establish purpose for reading (ss) | Visual schedule<br>Visuals accompanying text<br>General visual support from common items needed in class<br>Games to go along with text | Game playing<br>Movement | Built-in physical activity (i.e., fishing game) | Reading or game with peer | Data sheet for transitions | |

Between 8:05 and 8:20, Ginny completes independent morning work. The CAPS details supports for this task. For example, for morning work, Ginny is to complete five math problems that will result in her earning a break. A visual support is used to break down the task into its component parts, and sensory supports include a box that masks problems on the worksheet and a slant board that aids in writing. Data are collected by (a) Ginny through self-monitoring on following class rules posted in the room and (b) her teacher on completion of the five math problems. Self-monitoring was chosen for generalization and Ginny has asked to monitor her behavior at different times throughout the day. Figure 1.3 presents Ginny's CAPS and the materials that help her complete her daily tasks. This figure represents a mini-portfolio of Ginny's day. This pictorial representation serves multiple purposes:

1. It links the task to needed supports.

2. It provides a visual model for substitute teachers, paraeducators, and others who may work with Ginny throughout the day.

3. It can help Ginny's future teachers understand the supports that Ginny needed in each environment.

In this way, the CAPS, with supporting visual representations, ensures current and future success for Ginny at school.

## Figure 1.3. Ginny's CAPS showing support materials used.

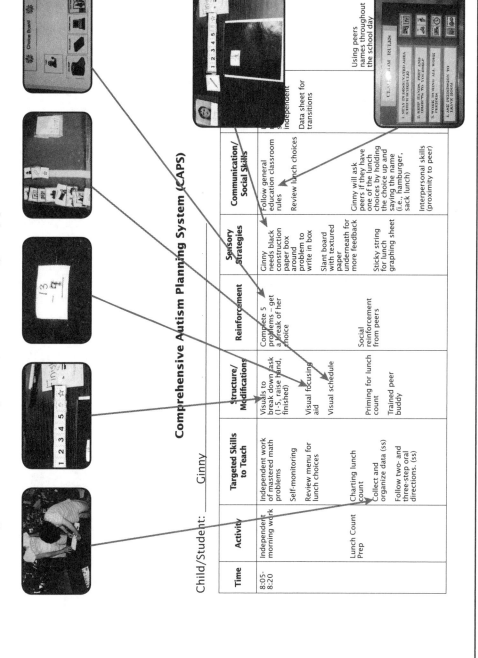

### Comprehensive Autism Planning System (CAPS)

Child/Student: _____ Ginny

| Time | Activity | Targeted Skills to Teach | Structure/ Modifications | Reinforcement | Sensory Strategies | Communication/ Social Skills |
|------|----------|--------------------------|--------------------------|---------------|--------------------|------------------------------|
| 8:05-8:20 | Independent morning work | Independent work of mastered math problems<br><br>Self-monitoring<br><br>Review menu for lunch choices | Visuals to break down (ask hand, raise hand, finished)<br><br>Visual focusing aid<br><br>Visual schedule | Complete 5 problems – get a break of her choice | Ginny needs black construction paper box around problem to write in box<br><br>Slant board with textured paper underneath for more feedback | Follow general education classroom rules<br><br>Review lunch choices |
| | Lunch Count Prep | Charting lunch count<br><br>Collect and organize data (ss)<br><br>Follow two- and three-step oral directions. (ss) | Priming for lunch count<br><br>Trained peer buddy | Social reinforcement from peers | Sticky string for lunch graphing sheet | Ginny will ask peers if they have one of the lunch choices by holding the choice up and saying the name (i.e., hamburger, sack lunch)<br><br>Interpersonal skills (proximity to peer) |

Data sheet for transitions

Using peers names throughout the school day

# Summary

The CAPS is a multifaceted system that allows educational professionals to know at a glance the goals for an activity and what students with ASD need to successfully engage in each activity. Completed by a team, CAPS can facilitate student independence across settings, activities, and people. This breakthrough tool supports compliance with the student's IEP and current legislation while reducing teacher's workload. Thus, the structure of this programming tool gives it broad applicability for children and youth with ASD.

# References

Aspy, R., & Grossman, B. G. (2007). *The Ziggurat model: A framework for designing comprehensive interventions for individuals with high-functioning autism and Asperger Syndrome.* Shawnee Mission, KS: Autism Asperger Publishing Company.

Frost, L., & Bondy, A. (2002). *The Picture Exchange Communication System training manual.* Newark, DE: Pyramid Educational Products.

# Structure/ Modifications

*Kai-Chien Tien, M.S., and Hyo Jung Lee, M.S.*

## CHAPTER 2

The potential of students with autism spectrum disorders (ASD) is often not realized because their learning style is not taken into consideration when planning and implementing educational programs. In addition, research has indicated that students with ASD require environmental as well as academic modifications in order to be successful. Research further supports that no one methodology is appropriate for all individuals on the autism spectrum (National Research Council, 2001; Tsatsanis, Foley, & Donebower, 2004).

This chapter will explore the intent behind CAPS's Structure/Modifications column (follows Time, Activity, and Targeted Skills to Teach in the model), which incorporates these considerations, thereby enhancing the possibility that the student's potential is fully realized.

## Environmental Considerations

It is well documented that students with ASD benefit from structure (cf., Ferguson, Myles, & Hagiwara, 2005; Panerai, Ferrante, & Zingale, 2002; Van Bourgondien, Reichle, & Schopler, 2003), especially when that structure includes visual supports (cf., Mesibov, Browder, & Kirkland, 2002; Morrison, Sainato, Benchaaban, & Endo, 2002; Stromer, Kimball, Kinney, & Taylor, 2006). Therefore, it is important to ensure that the environment is well organized and has a strong visual component.

***Classroom layout.*** All students benefit from a well-organized classroom. Indeed, a well-planned classroom can be as central to a student's success as any teaching or other intervention. Therefore, in order to create a classroom that is conducive to learning for students with ASD, teachers need to start by examining how the classroom space is organized.

As identified by Myles and Southwick (2005), components of a well-organized classroom include:

- Clearly defined areas for each activity

- Visual reminders of classroom expectations

- Adequate spacing to allow for personal space preferences, such as sitting at least 24" from another person

- Clear and consistent organization of materials, for example, by color coding and labeling (with written words, pictures, or both)

A well-organized environment is particularly beneficial for students with ASD as it provides the structure, predictability, and visual supports that many need. It informs them where to be, where to obtain items, where to return items, and what the classroom expectations are. Figure 2.1 provides an example of what a well-organized classroom may look like.

# Figure 2.1. Components of well-organized classrooms.

*Karla Dennis & Lezli Carson*

*Katie Lents*

*Rhonda Bowen, Marita Burrow, Jennifer Stanley, & Lisa Toler*

**Home base.** A home base is a quiet place in the school where students can go to (a) plan or review information or (b) cope with stress and behavioral challenges (Myles & Adreon, 2001; Myles & Southwick, 2005). It also serves as a place the student can go if (a) he feels the classroom is becoming overwhelming, (b) a teacher thinks a meltdown may be on the way, or (c) he needs a place to calm from overstimulation. There are no specific criteria for the location of a home base. Primarily, it should be a positive place for the student, and may be located anywhere that is quiet and comfortable, such as a resource room, a favorite teacher's classroom, or an ancillary staff member's office.

Home base is not a time-out, nor is it somewhere a student goes to escape work. Its use is individually determined. Some students primarily use the home base for coping with stress and behavioral challenges, whereas others use it on a regular basis to plan and review information. Time at home base can be scheduled into a student's school day and may be especially useful if scheduled immediately following a class period or activity that proves stressful for the student with ASD.

**Visual schedules.** Visual schedules take an abstract concept, such as time, and present it in a more concrete and manageable form. Visual schedules allow students to anticipate upcoming events and activities, develop an understanding of time, and facilitate the ability to predict change, thereby accommodating students' need for predictability and decreasing anxiety about the unknown.

Visual schedules can be created to present a range of information, from a student's daily schedule, to a schedule of activities that will be completed during each time period, to a schedule of activities that will be completed during a single task. The information listed in each schedule may be presented solely through words, through words and pictures, or entirely with pictures. The decision on what and how the information is presented should be based on the specific student's characteristics and preferences. Figure 2.2 provides a sample of a visual schedule for a student with ASD.

**Figure 2.2. Sample visual schedules.**

Boardmaker by Mayer-Johnson LLC. (1981-2005). *The Picture Communication Symbols*. All Rights Reserved Worldwide. Used with permission.

***Lists/task cards.*** Lists and task cards are valuable ways of presenting information to students with ASD by giving them something to refer back to. They may include information that would typically be presented only verbally, such as instructions, or information that would not be presented at all because it is assumed knowledge, such as the steps for handing in homework. Lists may include classroom rules and teacher expectations or test reminders. They break down tasks, such as assignments, into their component parts and set deadlines for their completion. Lists and task cards may be written in a variety of formats, from checklists to numbered lists of steps to be taken for completion of a task. Figure 2.3 shows an example of task cards.

**Figure 2.3. Sample task card.**

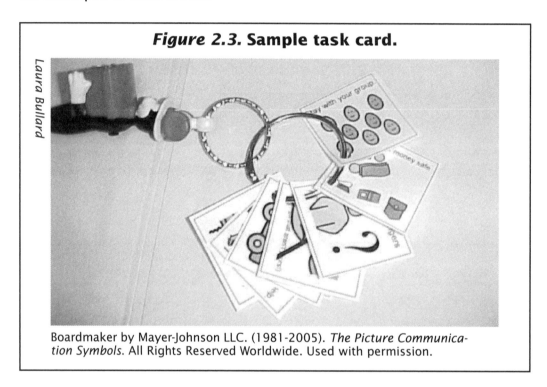

Laura Bullard

Boardmaker by Mayer-Johnson LLC. (1981-2005). *The Picture Communication Symbols*. All Rights Reserved Worldwide. Used with permission.

***Signals/cues.*** Signals and cues are subtle methods that adults use to prompt students to attend and respond. In addition, they can provide students with time needed to process information presented verbally. For example, John and Mrs. Wilcox have agreed that when the class discusses the answers to assignments and Mrs. Wilcox would like to call on John, she will:

- Walk by John's desk and tap his hand while saying, "Now let's talk about the answer for question number three."

- Pause.

- Call on John to share his answer to number three from last night's homework assignment.

***Choice boards.*** A verbal presentation of choices is often not effective with students with ASD. They may not listen to the whole message, may not be tuned into the message of all the choices, or may not re-member the choices presented. A choice board is an alternative way of presenting the choice possibilities by visually exhibiting them. The choices may be presented through pictures, through words, or through objects. Figure 2.4 is an example of a choice board.

*Figure 2.4.* **Sample choice board.**

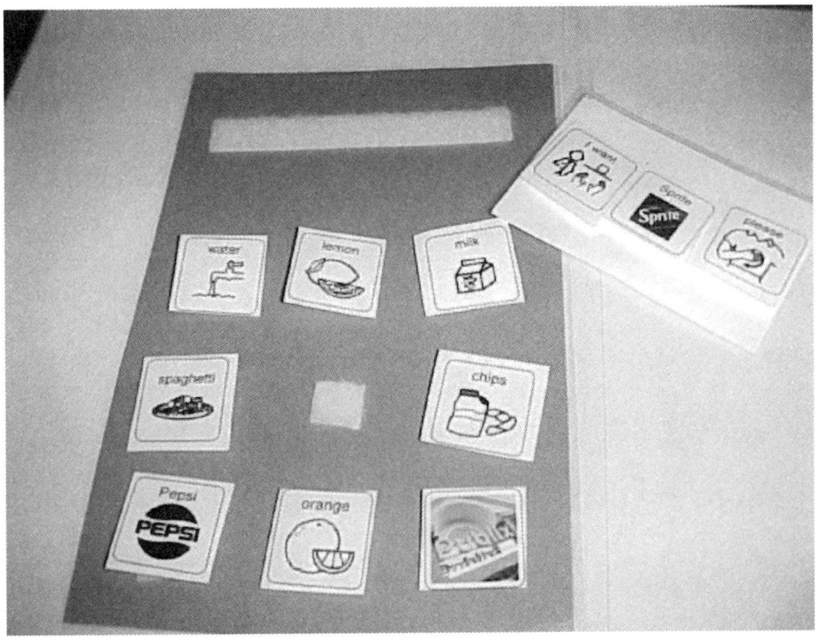

Boardmaker by Mayer-Johnson LLC. (1981-2005). *The Picture Communication Symbols.* All Rights Reserved Worldwide. Used with permission.

Using a choice board will aid and support student comprehension of the verbal message and choice situation. With a visual display, the student has time to see all the possible choices, to think about her response, and to check the options as frequently as she needs before making a decision. Taking the question "Do you want M&Ms or cookies?" as an example, the spoken message is delivered and over in a few seconds. A visual display of the choices, on the other hand, can be reviewed for an indefinite period and allows the student to think, comprehend, and make a choice. It further allows the student some control over certain situations and consequently reduces situational behavior problems.

*Boundary markers.* Boundary markers are strong visual cues that can be used throughout the classroom to guide students with ASD and their peers through physical spaces. Markers can be barriers, rugs, bookcases, other furniture, or colored tape on the floor that represent boundaries of areas for play and study.

*Early/late release.* Students with ASD are often extremely disrupted by transitions between classes or when going to special activities. Unanticipated schedule changes cause these students to experience high stress levels, and when this is combined with unfavorable environmental conditions such as lack of structure or boundaries, or too many visual distractions, the student is likely to have a meltdown, tantrum, cry, or refuse to comply.

These behavior problems are often the result of the student not knowing how to handle the situation. This may be circumvented by providing the student extra time to reach a destination. For example, releasing him 5 minutes before the bell rings or 5 minutes after the bell rings often brings about a relatively stress-free environment in which the student can get to a class, assembly, or other special event. This strategy may be particularly effective when combined with a transition buddy – a student who accompanies the child moving from one location to another.

# Academic Considerations

Most students with ASD require some sort of academic modifications. Modifications are diverse, ranging from altering the way in which materials are presented to modifying how children indicate competence of academic concepts. The following supports have been found particularly useful when programming for students with ASD.

*Graphic organizers.* Graphic organizers, such as semantic maps, Venn diagrams, outlines, and charts organize content material in a visual way that makes it easier to understand. They are valuable tools for helping students with ASD organize important information about a topic by providing visual and holistic representations of facts and concepts and their relationship within an organized framework. They are particularly useful with content-area material such as social studies, science, and so on.

Graphic organizers may be generated by hand and are also available from a number of sources, including paper templates, downloads from Web sites, and as components of computer programs. Figure 2.5 provides an example of a graphic organizer that may be effective for students with ASD.

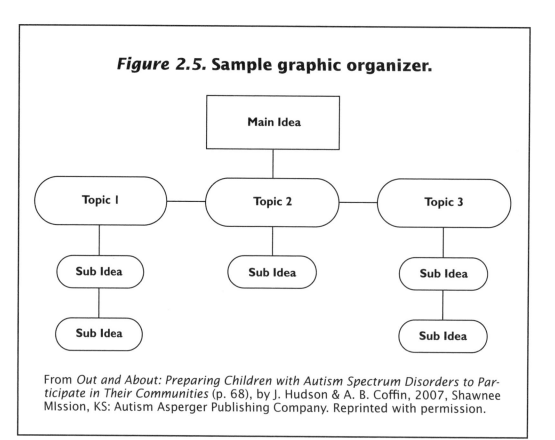

**Figure 2.5. Sample graphic organizer.**

From *Out and About: Preparing Children with Autism Spectrum Disorders to Participate in Their Communities* (p. 68), by J. Hudson & A. B. Coffin, 2007, Shawnee MIssion, KS: Autism Asperger Publishing Company. Reprinted with permission.

***Handwriting modifications.*** Individuals with Asperger Syndrome (AS) and high-functioning autism often have challenges with handwriting (Myles et al., 2003) that prevent them from adequately expressing what they know in writing (Myles & Adreon, 2001). The rule of thumb for identifying student competence has been stated as follows: "If you wish to know what a student with AS or high-functioning autism knows, do not ask her to write it down. A pencil in the hand typically means a concentration on the task of letter formation rather than the knowledge that the student needs to impart."

Alternatives to having the student write responses include (a) responding orally, (b) keyboarding, (c) answering questions in a true/false or multiple-choice format instead of an essay format, (d) reading answers into a tape recorder, or (e) using a scribe. In addition, occupational therapists can suggest accommodations for students who experience problems with handwriting.

***Assignment and test modifications.*** Similar to all other modifications, assignment and test modifications should match student need. For example, a student who works more slowly and methodically than peers may be allowed to complete fewer items. A student with handwriting issues may be allowed to do assignments or take tests verbally.

Many ways other than traditional assignment and test formats exist to assess students' knowledge. Examples include collages, crossword puzzles, interviews, posters, video presentations, etc. Table 2.1 offers several examples of assignment and test alternatives.

**Table 2.1**
***Alternatives to Traditional Assignments and Tests***

| Comic strip | Map |
|---|---|
| Graph or chart | Comic book |
| Riddles | Newspaper story |
| Scroll | Mural |
| Song or dance | Poem |
| Telegram | Timeline |
| Radio broadcast | Letter |
| Webcast | Banner |
| Webpage | Game |

Table 2.2 lists some potential modifications specific to tests that may benefit students with ASD.

## Table 2.2
### *Sample Test Modifications*

| | |
|---|---|
| Give a copy of the test beforehand | Allow responses to be drawn |
| Provide a practice test | Accept cursive handwriting or print |
| Test state/school objectives only | Have student tape record responses |
| Read test to the student | Give test in a quiet area |
| Allow the student to respond orally | Have the student rephrase incomplete answers |
| Use untimed tests | Allow the student to write on the test |
| Reduce number of items on the test | Avoid "bubble" tests that require answers to be transferred to a separate sheet of paper |
| Work a sample problem with the student | Allow the student to keyboard responses |
| Use a multiple-choice instead of essay format | Grade content, not mechanics |

***Notetaking strategies.*** Many students with ASD have difficulty when required to take notes in class. Often motor problems preclude getting important content onto paper in a timely manner. In addition, some students have difficulty listening and writing at the same time. Table 2.3 provides alternatives for typical notetaking.

As a prerequisite to teaching notetaking skills, teachers must first determine whether the student knows how to identify main ideas and supporting details. This is important, because quite often these skills are not directly taught, but assumed to be in place when students reach middle school.

---

**Table 2.3**
***Notetaking Alternatives***

- A teacher-developed complete outline that includes the main ideas and supporting details

- A teacher-developed skeletal outline that includes the main ideas and provides spaces for the student to fill in supporting details as these are discussed in class

- A peer-constructed outline developed by a fellow student using carbon paper or a photocopier

- Outlining software that allows the computer-adept student to take notes on main ideas and details

---

The first step in instruction is to teach the student to identify main ideas and details, in familiar written material. It is recommended that written rather than oral material be used because it is static and allows for visual review. In addition, familiar materials, such as materials related to a student's special interest, are used because they allow the student to focus on learning how to outline rather than on understanding new content.

---

*Leah had struggled to recognize main ideas and supporting details in social studies during the first nine weeks. When her teacher, Mr. Hardesty, decided to reintroduce these concepts to Leah using materials on her special interest, horses, she easily learned to identify main ideas and details.*

---

Once this step has been accomplished, students can begin the progression from using a teacher-developed complete outline to a skeletal outline. As mastery occurs, students gradually take more and more responsibility for outlining. The teacher facilitates this growing independence by teaching the student to recognize direct verbal cues that signal information that is important for the student to memorize and understand. A list of these phrases appears in Table 2.4.

*Mrs. Johnson taught Sam that when she said, "This is important," the item that followed was going to be on the weekly quiz.*

### Table 2.4
### *Sample Phrases That Indicate the Information Given Is Important*

- "This is important."
- "You need to remember ..."
- "The first main idea ..."
- "This is what started ..."
- "Remember these ..."
- "You need to understand ..."
- "Write this down."
- "This will be on the test."

Some students may not be able to progress past the skeletal outline stage. In such cases, providing the necessary materials, making outlining software available, or using peer-developed notes are viable ways of helping the student learn. In some classes, tape recording the lectures and providing the recording to students is beneficial.

**Priming.** Priming refers to the process of preparing the student for an activity that he will be expected to complete in the near future. Priming is strictly a preview of activities and an overview of assignments or schedule changes, instead of a time for teaching the academic content. Specifically, the student may be presented with the actual materials that will be used in class, such as a worksheet or outline for a group project, so that he knows what he will be working on in an upcoming class (Wilde, Koegel, & Koegel, 1992).

Given an opportunity to preview activities before they will occur, the student is often less likely to experience anxiety and stress about what lies ahead. With anxiety and stress at a minimum, the student can focus his efforts on successfully completing assignments and other activities.

Priming should occur close to when the target activity will occur. Priming may take place the day before an activity, the morning of the activity, the class period before, or even at the beginning of the class period during which the activity will be completed. It can occur at home or in school. Anyone can help the student with priming, a teacher, a parent, or peer. Priming should occur in short, concise time periods in an environment that is relaxing for the student with ASD.

# Multiple and Common Methodologies

CAPS is methodology-friendly. That is, it has the built-in flexibility to be used with almost any intervention approach. The categories within CAPS are directly related to research on the characteristics of children with ASD and effective interventions. In addition, the instructional goals, objectives, and standards that the child needs to meet may be drawn from any combination of the following: (a) norm-referenced assessment, (b) informal assessment, (c) functional behavior assessment, (d) direct observation, (e) state standards, and so forth. Instruction can be provided in a one-on-one, small-group, or large-group setting.

The National Autism Center (NAC; 2007) has developed a list of comprehensive treatment models along with criteria for their selection for students with ASD. CAPS can be used with each. Table 2.5 highlights some of the NAC-identified treatment models that are compatible with CAPS.

---

### Table 2.5
### *National Autism Center's Comprehensive Treatment Models and Associated Criteria*

A comprehensive treatment model is defined by five features:

1. It must be described in a refereed journal article, book chapter, or book that is commercially available to the public;

2. A set of procedural guides, manuals, or curricula exists to define the model;

3. It must have a clear theoretical or conceptual framework that is published in one of the formats noted previously;

4. The model must address multiple developmental or behavioral domains that, at a minimum, represent the core features of autism spectrum disorders (e.g., social competence, communication, repetitive behaviors);

5. The model must be intensive. Intensity is defined by the number of hours the model is implemented per week (i.e., National Academy of Sciences Committee recommended 25 hours or more), longevity (e.g., model implementation extends across a period equal to or greater than a typical school year, which is usually 9-10 months), and engagement (i.e., a planned set of activities or procedures actively engage the child/person with autism in learning experiences consistent with the model).

# Table 2.5 (cont.)

*Note.* For inclusion in this review, the comprehensive treatment model must have been implemented in the United States. An * next to the model name indicates that a peer-reviewed article describing program outcomes is available.

| Program Name | Representative Publication | Type of Publication |
|---|---|---|
| *Young Autism Project and Replication Sites | Lovaas, O. I. (1987). Behavioral treatment and normal educational and intellectual functioning in young autistic children. *Journal of Consulting and Clinical Psychology, 55,* 3-9. | Peer-reviewed journal article describing outcomes |
| *LEAP (Learning Experiences, and Alternative Program for Preschoolers and their Parents) | Strain, P., & Hoyson, M. (2000). The need for longitudinal intensive social skill intervention: LEAP follow-up outcomes for children with autism. *Topics in Early Childhood Special Education, 20,* 116-123. | Peer-reviewed journal article describing outcomes |
| *PCDI (Princeton Child Development Institute) | Fenske, E., Zalenski, S., Krantz, P., & McClannahan, L. (1985). Age at intervention and treatment outcome for autistic children in a comprehensive intervention program. *Analysis and Intervention in Developmental Disabilities, 5,* 49-58. | Peer-reviewed journal article describing outcomes |
| *Douglass Developmental Disabilities Center at Rutgers University | Handleman, J., Harris, S., Gordon, R., Kristoff, B., & Fuentes, F. (1991). Changes in cognitive and language functioning of preschool children with autism. *Journal of Autism and Developmental Disorders, 21,* 281-290. | Peer-reviewed journal article describing outcomes |
| *TEACCH (Treatment and Education of Autistic and related Communication-handicapped CHildren) | Panerai, S., Ferrante, L., & Zingale, M. (2002). Benefits of the Treatment and Education of Autistic and Communication Handicapped Children (TEACCH) programme as compared with a non-specific approach. *Journal of Intellectual Disability Research, 46,* 318-327. | Peer-reviewed journal article describing outcomes |
| *Denver Model | Rogers, S., & Lewis, H. (1988). An effective day treatment model for young children with pervasive developmental disorders. *Journal of the American Academy of Child and Adolescent Psychiatry, 28,* 207-214. | Peer-reviewed journal article describing outcomes |

## Table 2.5 (cont.)

| Program Name | Representative Publication | Type of Publication |
|---|---|---|
| *Children's Toddler School at Children's Health Center and Hospital, San Diego, CA | Stahmer, A., & Ingersoll, B. (2004). Inclusive programming for toddlers with autism spectrum disorders: Outcomes from the Children's Toddler School. *Journal of Positive Behavior Interventions*, 6, 67-82. | Peer-reviewed journal article describing outcomes |
| *Project DATA (Developmentally Appropriate Treatment for Autism) at University of Washington | Schwartz, I., Sandall, S., McBride, B., & Boulware, G. (2004). Project DATA (Developmentally Appropriate Treatment for Autism): An inclusive school-based approach to educating young children with autism. *Topics in Early Childhood Special Education*, 23, 156-168. | Peer-reviewed journal article describing outcomes |
| *River Street Autism Program, CT | Dyer, K., Martino, G., & Parvenski, T. (2006). The River Street Autism Program: A case study of a regional service center behavioral intervention program. *Behavior Modification*, 30, 925-943. | Peer-reviewed journal article describing outcomes |
| *Therapeutic Pathways, CA | Howard, J., Sparkman, C., Howard, C., Green, G., & Stanislaw, H. (2005). A comparison of intensive behavior analytic and eclectic treatments for young children with autism. *Research in Developmental Disabilities*, 26, 359-383. | Peer-reviewed journal article describing outcomes |
| *Daily Living Therapy (Higashi Model, Boston, MA) | Larkin, A., & Gurry, S. (1998). Progress reported in three children with autism using Daily Life Therapy. *Journal of Autism and Developmental Disorders*, 28, 339-342. | Peer-reviewed journal article describing outcomes |
| Walden Program, PA | McGee, G., Morrier, M., & Daly, T. (1999). An incidental teaching approach to early intervention for toddlers with autism. *The Journal of the Association for Persons with Severe Handicaps*, 24, 133-146. | Peer-reviewed journal article |
| Developmental, Individual-Difference, Relationship-Based model (DIR) | Greenspan, S., & Wieder, S. (1999). Developmental patterns and outcomes in infants and children with disorders in relating and communicating: A chart review of 200 cases of children with autistic spectrum disorders. *The Journal of Developmental and Learning Disorder*, 1, 87-141. | Book describing program written by model developers |

# Table 2.5 (cont.)

| Program Name | Representative Publication | Type of Publication |
|---|---|---|
| The Institute for Child Development (The Children's Unit) at State University of New York | The Children's Unit: Romanczyk, R. G., Lockshin, S., Gillis, J. M., & Matey, L. (2006). Institute for Child Development – preschool program. In S. Harris & J. Handleman (Eds.), *Preschool programs for children with autism* (3rd ed.). Austin, TX: Pro-Ed. | Book chapter describing model in book not edited by model developers |
| Autism Partnerships, CA | Leaf, R., McEachin, J., & Harsh, J. (1999). A work in progress: *Behavior management strategies and a curriculum for intensive behavioral treatment of autism.* New York: DRL Books. | Book describing procedures and curriculum by model developers |
| Relationship Development Intervention, TX | Gutstein, S., & Sheely, R. (2002). *Relationship Development Intervention with young children: Social and emotional development activities for Asperger syndrome, autism, PDD and NLD.* London: Jessica Kingsley Publishers. | Book describing procedures and curriculum by model developers |
| May Institute, MA | Luce, S., & Christian, W. (1989). State-of-the-art programming in Massachusetts: A brief description of the May Institute. In C. Gillberg (Ed.), *Diagnosis and treatment of autism.* New York: Plenum. | Book chapter describing model in book not edited by model developers |
| The SCERTS Model (Social Communication, Emotional Regulation, and Transactional Support) | Prizant, B., Wetherby, A., Rubin, E., Laurent, A., & Rydell, P. (2005). *The SCERTS™ Model: A comprehensive educational approach for children with autism spectrum disorders.* Baltimore: Brookes. | Book describing procedures and curriculum by model developers |
| Pivotal Response Treatment | Koegel, L. K., Koegel, R. L., Shoshan, Y., & McNerney, E. (1999). Pivotal response intervention II: Preliminary long-term outcomes data. *Journal of the Association for Persons with Severe Handicaps, 24,* 186-198. | Journal article describing procedures by model developers |
| Alpine Learning Group, NJ | Meyer, L., Taylor, B., Cerion, K., Fisher, J., Moran, L., & Richard, E. (2006). Alpine Learning Group. In J. Handleman & S. Harris (Eds.), *School age education programs for children with autism.* Austin, TX: Pro-Ed. | Book chapter describing model in book not edited by model developers |

## Table 2.5 (cont.)

| Program Name | Representative Publication | Type of Publication |
|---|---|---|
| Lancaster-Lebanon Intermediate Unit 13, PA | Bruey, C. & Vorhis, N. (2006). The Lancaster-Lebanon IU 13 autistic support program. In J. Handleman & S. Harris (Eds.), *School age education programs for children with autism*. Austin, TX: Pro-Ed. | Book chapter describing model in book not edited by model developers |
| The Pyramid Approach, DE | Bondy, A., & Battaglini, K. (2006). Application of the pyramid approach to education model in a public school setting. In J. Handleman & S. Harris (Eds.), *School age education programs for children with autism*. Austin, TX: Pro-Ed. | Book chapter describing model in book not edited by model developers |
| Summit Academy, NY | Anderson, S., Thomeer, M., & King, D. (2006). Summit Academy: Implementing a system wide intervention. In J. Handleman & S. Harris (Eds.), *School age education programs for children with autism*. Austin, TX: Pro-Ed. | Book chapter describing model in book not edited by model developers |
| The Valley Program, NJ | McKeon, J., Vuoncino, K., Brenkert, R., Dinnell-LoPresti, K., Doyle, E., Lampert, M., Madden-Perez, M., & Rossig, S. (2006). The Valley Program. In J. Handleman & S. Harris (Eds.), *School age education programs for children with autism*. Austin, TX: Pro-Ed. | Book chapter describing model in book not edited by model developers |
| Verbal Behavior | Partington, J. (2005). *The updated ABLLS: The Assessment of Basic Language and Learning Skills*. Pleasant Hill, CA: Behavior Analysts Inc. | Book describing curriculum by model developer |
| Eden Model, NJ | Holmes, D. (1998). *Autism through the lifespan: The Eden model*. Bethesda, MD: Woodbine House. | Book describing curriculum by model developer |
| Comprehensive Occupational Therapy Approach | Miller-Kuhaneck. H. (2004). *Autism: A comprehensive occupational therapy approach*. Bethesda, MD: American Occupational Therapy Association | Book describing procedures and curriculum by model developers |
| STAR Program, OR | Arick, J., Krug, D., Loos, L., & Falco, R. (2005). School-based programs. In F. Volkmar, R. Paul, A. Klin, & D. Cohen (Eds.), *Handbook of autism and pervasive developmental disorders*. Hoboken, NJ: John Wiley & Sons. | Book chapter describing model in book not edited by model developers |

From National Autism Center, www.nationalautismcenter.org. Reprinted with permission.

# Summary

Structure/modifications are essential components of the CAPS model. Environmental and academic supports can help students across the spectrum show their competence. Moreover, CAPS supports matching students to the methodology/ies used to enhance their achievement across their day.

# References

Ferguson, H., Myles, B. S., & Hagiwara, T. (2005). Using a personal digital assistant to enhance the independence of an adolescent with Asperger syndrome. *Education and Training in Developmental Disabilities, 40*, 60-67.

Mesibov, G. B., Browder, D. M., & Kirkland, C. (2002). Using individualized schedules as a component of positive behavioral support for students with developmental disabilities. *Journal of Positive Behavior Interventions, 4*, 73-79.

Morrison, R. S., Sainato, D. M., Benchaaban, D., & Endo, S. (2005). Increasing play skills of children with autism using activity schedules and correspondence training. *Journal of Early Intervention, 25*, 58-72.

Myles, B. S., & Adreon, D. (2001). *Asperger Syndrome and adolescence: Practical solutions for school success.* Shawnee Mission, KS: Autism Asperger Publishing Company.

Myles, B. S., Huggins, A., Rome-Lake, M., Hagiwara, T., Barnhill, G. P., & Griswold, D. E. (2003). Written language profile of children and youth with Asperger Syndrome. *Education and Training in Developmental Disabilities, 38*(4), 362-370.

Myles, B. S., & Southwick, J. (2005). *Asperger Syndrome and difficult moments: Practical solutions for tantrums, rage, and meltdowns* (2nd ed.). Shawnee Mission, KS: Autism Asperger Publishing Company.

43

National Autism Center. (2007). *National Autism Center's comprehensive treatment models and associated criteria.* Boston, MA: Author.

National Research Council. (Ed.). (2001). *Educating children with autism.* Washington, DC: National Academy Press.

Paneri, S., Ferrante, L., & Zingale, M. (2002). Benefits of the Treatment and Education of Autistic and Communication Handicapped Children (TEACCH) programme as compared with a non-specific approach. *Journal of Intellectual Disability Research, 46*(4), 318-327.

Stromer, R., Kimball, J. W., Kinney, E. M., & Taylor, B. A. (2006). Activity schedules, computer technology, and teaching children with autism spectrum disorders. *Focus on Autism and Other Developmental Disabilities, 21,* 14-24.

Tsatsanis, K. D., Foley, C., & Donebower, C. (2004). Contemporary outcome research and programming guidelines for Asperger syndrome and high-functioning autism. *Topics in Language Disorders, 24,* 249-259.

Van Bourgondien, M. E., Reichle, N. C., & Schopler, E. (2003). Effects of a model treatment approach on adults with autism. *Journal of Autism and Developmental Disorders, 33,* 131-140.

Wilde, L. D., Koegel, L. K., & Koegel, R. L. (1992). *Increasing success in school through priming: A training manual.* Santa Barbara: University of California.

# Reinforcement

*Joyce Downing, Ph.D.*

## CHAPTER 3

**W**hat is reinforcement? When and how do we use it? Teachers and parents often use the term "reinforcement" informally, describing a variety of ways to reward children for completing their assigned tasks or chores. For the purposes of this book, reinforcement involves delivering a specific consequence when a student demonstrates a target behavior to increase the likelihood that the behavior will occur again when requested.

Based in the well-researched fields of experimental analysis of behavior (EAB) and applied behavior analysis (ABA; Cooper, Heron, & Heward, 2007), reinforcement is more than just a reward; it is a powerful tool for teaching and maintaining desirable academic, communicative, and social behaviors. This chapter will discuss how to identify and use reinforcement most effectively as part of the Comprehensive Autism Planning System (CAPS).

---

### Definition of Reinforcement

Reinforcement involves delivering a specific consequence when the student demonstrates a target behavior to increase the likelihood that the behavior will occur again when requested.

# Selecting Reinforcers: Specific Consequences

Natural environments provide a variety of potential reinforcers, including the approval of peers and adults, access to preferred activities or objects, and opportunities to make choices. "Commonly used classroom reinforcement strategies include verbal praise, approving gestures (nods, smiles, winks, thumbs-up), positive physical touch (pat on shoulder, high-five), individual feedback and recognition, positive individual attention, and individual and group tangibles" (Downing, 2007, p. 100).

As part of CAPS, reinforcers must be selected carefully, based on the student's needs and characteristics. For example, Billy may find a high-five for completing his work very reinforcing, but for Adrienne, who is preoccupied with germs and avoids casual physical contact, it would likely have an adverse effect.

A reinforcer may be positive (giving a reward) or negative (taking away or reducing something aversive). The reinforcer can be social, or tangible, or part of a generalized system that is used for the entire class. Regardless of type, it must be something the student is willing to work for. The reinforcer should be selected in advance, and delivered as soon as the student has demonstrated the requested behavior.

Table 3.1 includes an array of potential reinforcers by category or type. While some students will work for the same reinforcer every day, most prefer a range of options. A reinforcer menu for individual students or groups can be developed by a variety of informal strategies, including (a) observing preferences and choices in natural settings, (b) asking the students what they would like to work for, or (c) interviewing parents or teachers to determine what has worked in the past (cf., DeLeon & Iwata, 1996; Didden, deMoor, & Bruyns, 1997; Fisher, Piazza, Bowman, & Amari, 1996).

| Table 3.1 Potential Reinforcers by Category | | |
|---|---|---|
| **Social/Activity** | **Tangible/Edible** | **Generalized/Token System** |
| <ul><li>Take a break</li><li>Play a game</li><li>Use the computer</li><li>Spend time with a preferred individual</li><li>Put name on the "brag board"</li><li>Earn 5-minute break for the whole class</li><li>Skip one assignment</li><li>Obtain a high-status privilege (feed the goldfish for the day)</li></ul> | <ul><li>Healthy snack or beverage (e.g., raisins, fruit jerky, cereal)</li><li>"Cool" school supplies (e.g., Batman eraser)</li><li>Small toy</li><li>Baseball card or other trading card</li><li>Inexpensive jewelry or grooming items</li><li>Certificates, ribbons, badges</li><li>CDs, videogames</li></ul> | <ul><li>Points</li><li>Play money</li><li>Gold stars</li><li>Stickers</li><li>Tickets, coupons</li><li>Poker chips</li><li>Marbles in a jar to earn class pizza party</li></ul> *Note: In the token system, the actual reinforcers are chosen from a menu of items similar to those in Columns 1 and 2.* |

Another way to select reinforcers, as well as to identify replacement behaviors, is to consider the function of the student's problem behavior. Most behaviors are instrumental; that is, students are often attempting to either "get" or "get out of" something. For example, students may be attempting to secure the attention of their peers or adults, obtain a tangible object, or gain access to a desired activity. They may refuse to engage in activities they find stressful or difficult, or they may avoid interaction with specific individuals. For students with limited communication skills, including those with ASD who in times of stress have a limited ability to communicate, behavior may be an effort to address their needs and wants. In some cases, problem behavior may be related to sensory processing, as students attempt to manage their sensory input (for further information, see Chapter 4).

*The role of the team is to develop a hypothesis about why problem behavior occurs, based on patterns of classroom behavior. The hypothesis can be used to select replacement behaviors and reinforcers that address the function – or purpose – of the behavior in more acceptable ways.*

For example, Johnny routinely fell to the floor during science class. The autism specialist, Ms. Teen, observed Johnny during science class as well as during other classes. A careful analysis of the environment led her to believe that his behavior might be related to the teacher writing on the whiteboard with a marker.

Ms. Teen met with the team, and they hypothesized that the sound of the marker on the board might be discomforting to Johnny. The occupational therapist suggested providing Johnny with earplugs during the times the teacher wrote on the board; the teacher suggested that she could try to do all writing on the board before class began. Both strategies were tested and were determined to be effective, with the former being most consistently effective.

Table 3.2 provides a list of potential reinforcers for students whose behavior appears to represent an effort to gain sensory input.

## Table 3.2
### *Potential Sensory Reinforcers*

| Auditory | Visual | Olfactory |
|---|---|---|
| <ul><li>Bells, chimes</li><li>Recorded music</li><li>Animal sounds</li><li>Running or bubbling water (e.g., fountain, fish tank)</li><li>Whistles, flutes, rainsticks, musical instruments</li><li>White noise</li></ul> | <ul><li>Battery-operated or windup toys</li><li>Nature videos</li><li>Animated computer screen savers</li><li>Kaleidoscopes, prisms, mirrors</li><li>Colorful pinwheels</li><li>Adjust lights (brighter, dimmer, colored)</li></ul> | <ul><li>Potpourri</li><li>Candles</li><li>Hand lotion</li><li>Body oil</li><li>Perfume</li><li>Air freshener</li><li>Scented crayons or markers</li><li>Scratch and sniff stickers</li></ul> |
| **Taste/Oral Motor** | **Tactile** | **Proprioceptive/Vestibular** |
| <ul><li>Crunchy foods</li><li>Chewy snacks or gum</li><li>Sweet or sour snacks or liquids</li><li>Suckers</li><li>Blowing bubbles, whistles, straws, balloons</li></ul> | <ul><li>Tickles and bear hugs</li><li>Petting a dog or cat</li><li>Holding something cold or hot</li><li>Stroking or rubbing skin with textured materials (e.g., fur, chenille, baby hairbrush)</li></ul> | <ul><li>Rocking chair</li><li>Sit-and-Spin™</li><li>Swing</li><li>Trampoline, pogo stick</li><li>Structured exercise (weights, bicycle, aerobics)</li><li>Grip-strengthening tools (stress balls, etc.)</li></ul> |

# Delivering Reinforcement

The reinforcement must be *contingent* on the target behavior; that is, the student only earns the predetermined consequence *if and when* she performs the requested behavior. The target behavior must also be clearly defined and include a measurable criterion that easily determines whether the student has earned the reinforcer. Vaguely defined target behaviors and unclear criteria are likely to result in confusion and power struggles as the student and adult attempt to negotiate their understanding of the plan. In the sample CAPS in Chapter 1, Ginny can earn a break when she has completed five math problems. If she refuses to complete the assignment, or only completes three math problems, Ginny does not earn the reward. In this example, "Completing math problems" is the target behavior and "five problems" is the criterion.

***Measuring criteria.*** The criterion can be measured by a variety of methods. In the example above, Ginny's success was determined by the number of math problems she completed. Sometimes the criterion is expressed as duration, or the length of time necessary to complete the task. For example, "Using her visual schedule, Ginny will transition to her reading group in less than 3 minutes." For some behaviors, success may be expressed as a percent correct or a percentage of time elapsed. For example, "Ginny will remain in her seat at least 80% of the time during independent seatwork." The initial criterion should be based on the student's present level of educational performance and adjusted incrementally only after the student has demonstrated mastery of the desired behavior. For Ginny, that might mean rewarding transition to reading group at the 3-minute level for five consecutive days, then adjusting the criteria to 2.75 minutes for five days, and so on.

Vaguely defined target behaviors and unclear criteria are likely to result in confusion and power struggles as the student and adult attempt to negotiate their understanding of the plan.

***Schedule of systems.*** Another important consideration is the schedule of reinforcement used. When teaching a new behavior to mastery, or introducing a replacement behavior to address a problem, reinforcement is generally delivered on a one-to-one (1:1) basis. That means that for every instance of the target behavior, the student receives the reinforcer. After the student has demonstrated fluency in the new skill, the ratio of behaviors to reinforcer can be raised gradually.

***Reinforcement systems.*** For older or high-functioning students, classwide reinforcement systems such as point systems and token economies may be useful. These generalized systems allow teachers to establish a common menu of social, activity, and tangible rewards that can be used with a group of students with differing needs and preferences. Rather than receiving reinforcement immediately, students earn tokens that have no actual value (points, coupons, play money) but that can be exchanged later for their choice of backup reinforcers from the menu.

# Troubleshooting

The purpose of reinforcement is to teach and support appropriate behavior. Therefore, if the desired behavior does not occur when requested, the team needs to consider the following questions and adjust the reinforcement plan based on their conclusions:

- **Were the task requirements and the selected consequence clearly stated by the adult and understood by the student?** If not, then reteach or restructure the task, and check for understanding. Example: Ginny begins whining when asked to begin her math problems. Use a visual support to cue Ginny that when she finishes her five problems, she will earn a break (see Figure 3.1 for Ginny's work system). As she finishes each problem, the icon can be checked off or covered with a sticker.

---

**Figure 3.1. Ginny's work system.**

| $\frac{\begin{array}{r}2\\+3\end{array}}{5}$ | $\frac{\begin{array}{r}2\\+3\end{array}}{5}$ | $\frac{\begin{array}{r}2\\+3\end{array}}{5}$ | $\frac{\begin{array}{r}2\\+3\end{array}}{5}$ | $\frac{\begin{array}{r}2\\+3\end{array}}{5}$ | breaktime |

---

- **Was the target behavior a task the student could perform without prompting?** If not, consider adding a verbal prompt or precorrection to your request. Example: Ginny sometimes becomes confused and agitated when it is time for her to transition to her reading group. Use a visual cue to remind Ginny to refer to her visual schedule (see Figure 3.2). When Ginny brings you her schedule, say, "What's next? Reading. Good job."

---

**Figure 3.2. Cue to check visual schedule.**

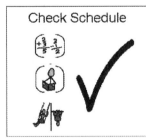

- **Was the reinforcer chosen by the student and sufficiently desirable?** If not, work with the student to identify a reinforcer that is stronger or allow a choice between two options. Example: Ginny does not respond to a teacher request. Present Ginny with pictures or icons representing two preferred activities or tangibles. Ask, "Ginny, what do you want to work for?" Place the picture she has selected next to her break icon.

- **Was the reinforcer delivered immediately following the target behavior?** If not, consider strategies to either reduce the student's wait time or increase the student's tolerance for waiting. Example: Ginny finishes her math problems, but the teacher is busy with another student and cannot tend to Ginny right away. Ginny becomes agitated. Teach Ginny to use a Wait Card (see Figure 3.3) and get to her as quickly as possible. Hand her the card and say, "Wait, please." For more information on teaching the wait strategy, see Frost and Bondy (2002).

---

*Figure 3.3.* **Visual cue for wait.**

# wait

Boardmaker by Mayer-Johnson LLC. (1981-2005). *The Picture Communication Symbols.* All Rights Reserved Worldwide. Used with permission. www.mayer-johnson.com

- **If the desired behavior replaced a previous problem behavior, did the replacement behavior and reinforcer address the function of the student's original behavior?** If not, consider adjusting the plan to find a better fit for the functional hypothesis. Example: Ginny can earn raisins for moving between classrooms without screeching. The team believes the screeching is Ginny's way of communicating her anxiety about the noise and proximity of other students in the hall. Neither the desired behavior (walking down the hall quietly) nor the reinforcer (raisins) has addressed Ginny's need to communicate or her anxiety.

Stress-reduction strategies might include (a) providing a passing time that reduces the number of other students in the hall, (b) developing a visual cue card that allows Ginny to communicate her concerns to an adult (see Figure 3.4), or (c) giving Ginny a stress ball to squeeze when she feels like screeching. Finally, a function-related reinforcer might be for Ginny to sit on the beanbag listening to music through headphones after reaching her destination.

***Figure 3.4.* Visual cue for noisy.**

noisy

Boardmaker by Mayer-Johnson LLC. (1981-2005). *The Picture Communication Symbols*. All Rights Reserved Worldwide. Used with permission. www.mayer-johnson.com

# Summary

Research has unequivocally shown that reinforcement is an essential component in learning (Cooper et al., 2007; Didden et al., 1997). In fact, according to Aspy and Grossman (2007), without reinforcement there is no learning. CAPS supports this concept by ensuring that reinforcement is considered throughout the student's day.

# References

Aspy, R., & Grossman, B. G. (2007). *The Ziggurat model: A framework for designing comprehensive interventions for individuals with high-functioning autism and Asperger Syndrome.* Shawnee Mission, KS: Autism Asperger Publishing Company.

Cooper, J. O., Heron, T. E., & Heward, W. L. (2007). *Applied behavior analysis* (2nd ed.). Upper Saddle River, NJ: Pearson Education.

DeLeon, I., & Iwata, B. A. (1996). Evaluation of a multiple-stimulus presentation format for assessing reinforcer preferences. *Journal of Applied Behavior Analysis, 29*, 519-533.

Didden, R., deMoor, J. M., & Bruyns, W. (1997). Effectiveness of DRO tokens in decreasing disruptive behaviors in the classroom with five multiply handicapped children. *Behavioral Interventions, 12*, 65-75.

Downing, J. A. (2007). *Students with emotional and behavioral problems: Assessment, management and intervention strategies.* Saddle River, NJ: Merrill/Prentice Hall.

Fisher, W. W., Piazza, C. C., Bowman, L. G., & Amari, A. (1996). Integrating caregiver report with a systematic choice assessment to enhance reinforcer identification. *American Journal on Mental Retardation, 101*, 15-25.

Frost, L., & Bondy, A. (2002). *The Picture Exchange Communication System training manual* (2nd ed.). Newark: DE: Pyramid Educational Products.

# Sensory Strategies

## CHAPTER 4

Although not specified as a characteristic of autism spectrum disorders (ASD) in the *Diagnostic and Statistical Manual of Mental Disorders* (4th Edition, Text Revision; DSM-IV, TR; American Psychiatric Association [APA, 2000]), sensory issues appear to be inherent in individuals with this exceptionality.

While the research base on sensory characteristics in ASD is limited, several empirical investigations have been conducted in this area. For example, Rogers and Ozonoff (2005) identified 48 studies on sensory issues in autism revealing that individuals on the spectrum have significant challenges in this area. Even less research has been conducted relative to high-functioning autism (HFA) or Asperger Syndrome (AS) in all areas, not just sensory. However, evidence exists to show that sensory challenges are also apparent in this part of the spectrum (Dunn, Myles, & Orr, 2002; Gepner & Mestre, 2002; Green et al., 2002; Myles, Hagiwara et al., 2004: Pfeiffer, Kinnealey, Reed, & Herzberg, 2005).

While not considered by some (cf. National Research Council, 2001) as an evidence-based practice, the argument can be made that sensory-based strategies can at least be identified as promising.

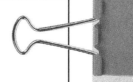

Again, while not extensive, research has also been conducted on sensory interventions for individuals with ASD. For example, in 2002, Baranek identified 22 studies conducted on sensory and motor interventions. Additional studies have been conducted since that time (cf., Kaplan, Clopton, Kaplan, Messbauer, & McPherson, 2006; Myles, Simpson et al., 2004; Schilling & Schwartz, 2004). While not considered by some (cf. National Research Council, 2001) as an evidence-based practice, the argument can be made that sensory-based strategies can at least be identified as promising.

Using this base of information as a foundation, this chapter will begin with a brief overview of the sensory system and how it impacts individuals with ASD and conclude with some sensory-based strategies as they relate to creating support via the CAPS.

# The Sensory Systems

Our body has seven individual sensory systems, tactile, vestibular, proprioceptive, visual, auditory, gustatory, and olfactory, each of which is the starting point for delivering messages to the central nervous system for further processing. Table 4.1 shows an overview of the functions of each system.

## Table 4.1
### *Location and Functions of the Sensory Systems*

| System | Location | Function |
|---|---|---|
| Tactile (touch) | Skin – density of cell distribution varies throughout the body. Areas of greatest density include mouth, hands, and genitals. | Provides information about the environment and qualities of objects (touch, pressure, texture, hard, soft, sharp, dull, heat, cold, pain). |
| Vestibular (balance) | Inner ear – stimulated by head movements and input from other senses, especially visual. | Provides information about where our body is in space, and whether or not we or our surroundings are moving. Tells about speed and direction of movement. |
| Proprioception (body awareness) | Muscles and joints – activated by muscle contractions and movement. | Provides information about where a certain body part is and how it is moving. |
| Visual (sight) | Eye retina – stimulated by light. | Provides information about objects and persons. Helps us define boundaries as we move through time and space. |
| Auditory (hearing) | Inner ear – stimulated by air/sound waves. | Provides information about sounds in the environment (loud, soft, high, low, near, far). |
| Gustatory (taste) | Chemical receptors in the tongue – closely entwined with the olfactory (smell) system. | Provides information about different types of taste (sweet, sour, bitter, salty, spicy). |
| Olfactory (smell) | Chemical receptors in the nasal structure – closely associated with the gustatory system. | Provides information about different types of smell (musty, acrid, putrid, flowery, pungent). |

From *Asperger Syndrome and Sensory Issues: Practical Solutions for Making Sense of the World* (p. 5), by B. S. Myles, K. T. Cook, N. E. Miller, L. Rinner, & L. Robbins, 2000, Shawnee Mission, KS: Autism Asperger Publishing Company. Reprinted with permission.

Some parts of the body have an increased density or number of receptors compared to other parts. For example, the mouth and hands have relatively more receptors than the arms or legs and, therefore, are often more sensitive to sensory input such as touch and temperature.

# The Sensory Integration Process

In order to "make sense" of all the sensations we experience, we must integrate them.

1. First, we register or become aware of the sensation.

2. Then we orient or pay attention to it.

3. Next, we attempt to interpret the sensation by using current information and referencing past experiences for comparison.

4. Organization occurs when our brain decides what we should do in response to the sensation.

5. The final step is execution, or what we actually do.

Table 4.2 provides a graphic of this process. These steps can occur in less than one second, and since they happen in a quick and flowing manner, we are typically not aware of the individual stages.

# Table 4.2
## *The Sensory Integration Process*

 **Registration:** This the point at which we know we have tasted, touched, smelled, or heard something. We all have different awareness levels (called thresholds) for different sensory stimuli. The person who can hear something that others cannot may be said to have a low auditory threshold. Threshold also varies based on time of day, emotional state, physical health, genetic predisposition, past experiences, etc.

 **Orientation:** At this stage, we focus on the sensory input by attending, touching, smelling, etc. Basically, the brain tells us what to attend to or what to ignore.

 **Interpretation:** Interpretation involves linking the present sensory experience to a past experience. Past experiences include emotions, thoughts, memories, conversations, etc. The term, "fright, flight, or fight" is associated with interpretation.

 **Organization:** During this stage, we decide if we need to respond to the stimuli and what, if any, response we need to make.

 **Execution:** This is the action (or lack of action) stage where we carry out a response or decide not to react.

# Discriminative and Protective Functions

When we have a sensory experience, the brain interprets the experience in one of two ways: discriminative or protective. These two functions form the basis for future sensory experiences.

Each system has a *discriminative component* that supplies details for the central nervous system to consider. For example, when a person touches (tactile) an object, the tactile system provides information about where the touch is occurring (on the hand, not on the head) as well as whether the object is hard, soft, fuzzy, smooth, round, angular, etc. Accurate information about these attributes helps us interpret the object so that we can respond appropriately.

The sensory systems also have a *protective function* that helps to protect us from harm. For example, when we reach into a shoe and detect something soft and fuzzy, the tactile system may signal us to move our hand quickly to keep from being bitten by a spider.

The central nervous system is designed to help the body maintain a state of equilibrium or balance to ensure that we can think, problem solve, and make decisions. If sensory information starts to interfere with equilibrium, the neurological system may generate a protective "fright, flight, or fight" reaction, often accompanied by physiological responses to support survival from other parts of the body,

> Sensory inputs have the potential to evoke a number of reactions that we typically call behavior.

such as sweating, dilation of pupils, or an increased heart rate. Sensory inputs have the potential to evoke a number of reactions that we typically call behavior. In other words, the behaviors that we see (and don't see) in somebody come from what and how that person sees, feels, hears, or otherwise senses.

# Modulation

*Modulation*, a term often used by occupational therapists (OT), refers to the ability to balance or regulate the sensory systems. Inherent in modulation is:

- awareness that your system is out of balance with the environment

- recognition of the response that is appropriate to the environment

- knowledge of strategies that can recreate the necessary balance.

For example, when you start to feel tired on a long drive, you might chew gum, drink something cold, or turn up the radio to become more alert. Conversely, to calm your child before going to bed, you might read her a story, give her a warm bath, or play a quiet game.

# Effective and Ineffective Sensory Processing

Most of the time, the sensory integration process is very effective. That is, we take in information, process it, and act on it appropriately. We register, orient, interpret, organize, and execute a response in a manner that is well matched to the situation. The brain's regulation or modulation of sensory messages supports that effective performance by further integrating this information to result in a behavior or action that matches our intent.

Individuals with ineffective sensory processing can experience problems in one or more of the sensory areas or at any point in the sensory integration process. Difficulties with effective registration of sensory input disrupt subsequent steps in the integration process. For example, if orientation toward a particular sensory stimulus does not occur, it cannot be interpreted, and so on. Poor modulation of input may result in over- or under-reaction. That is, responses that are not balanced to meet the situation.

***Examples of effective sensory processing.*** Children who process sensory information effectively tend to be responsive to home routines, manage successfully on community outings, and are frequently viewed favorably by teachers in the school setting. Such children:

- can continue their play in the yard without being bothered by the noise of the lawn mower, weeder, and edge trimmer

- eat a variety of foods although certain preferences may be evident

- accompany their parents as they make their way through the crowd to find a place at the curb to wait for the parade to begin without reacting to the close proximity of other people

- tolerate the singing and dancing of the staff entertaining at the restaurant where Grandma and Grandpa take them

- finish their seatwork because they do not orient toward the noises of children on the playground

- complete their assignments because they follow verbal directions and can sit for an extended period of time

- identify a source of information (such as a teacher), orient toward that information and attend, differentiating irrelevant from relevant information

- work on a assignment while "tuning out" background noises in the classroom, such as a pencil tapping, someone coughing, two children whispering.

As these examples indicate, a child with effective sensory processing is ready to learn

> Individuals with ineffective sensory processing can experience problems in one or more of the sensory areas or at any point in the sensory integration process.

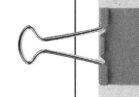

and demonstrate that knowledge.

***Evidence of ineffective sensory processing.*** On the other hand, children who have sensory processing difficulties often experience challenges in home, community, and school settings. This might be seen in children who:

- cannot tolerate tags on shirts

- startle easily and do not readily calm afterward

- avoid playground equipment

- cover their ears or scream with sudden loud noises, such as a vacuum cleaner or the toilet flushing

- react strongly when someone brushes against them in line

- cannot tolerate the smell of fabric softener on a peer's shirt

- look at the teacher when she talks, but have difficulty screening out irrelevant stimuli, such as the buzz of the fluorescent lights

- have difficulty with activities that involve motor planning, such as participating in sports, carrying a lunch tray, opening a milk carton, tying shoes, or riding a bicycle

- have difficulty writing with a pencil or pen because they cannot tell how much pressure to apply to hold the writing implement or experience discomfort when gripping it.

Children with sensory processing challenges are often not available to learn. They are bothered by seemingly minor stimuli that others ignore; they cannot concentrate; and once upset, they cannot inherently self-calm. Ineffective sensory processing can be a strong factor in a child's academic or social failure.

# Sensory Interventions

An OT can be effective in identifying and designing sensory supports that can assist a child with ASD in meeting the needs of the environment, such as attending to the teacher, completing her assignments, or playing on playground equipment. Following an assessment of (a) the child's sensory needs, (b) the behavior the child exhibits, and (c) what is expected in the environment, the OT can plan interventions that can fit into the child's CAPS.

It is important that an OT trained in sensory integration design interventions because specific types of sensory input can remain in the system for extended periods of time. Indeed, inappropriate use of or a miscalculation of the length or onset of an intervention could result in actual physical harm to the child. Table 4.3 outlines the time that input of each sensory system stays in a child's system (Brack, 2004).

> Ineffective sensory processing can be a strong factor in a child's academic or social failure.

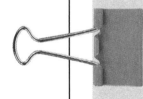

This supports the notion that sensory supports must match the child's need and be embedded into to the child's schedule. For example, if a child's attention is enhanced through oral-motor input, he might need gum, pretzels, or a straw to chew on throughout the day. An OT can consult with a child's teacher to ensure that these supports are available when needed. Thus, the child can be immersed in a sensory-friendly environment where learning is likely to occur.

**Table 4.3**
**_Length of Time Sensory Input Stays in the System_**

| Sensory System | Length of Time the Input Stays in the System |
|---|---|
| Tactile | 1 to 1.5 hours |
| Vestibular | 4 to 8 hours |
| Proprioception | 1 to 1.5 hours |
| Visual | Only when sensory input is presented (e.g., visual only works when the child sees it) |
| Auditory | Only when sensory input is presented |
| Gustatory | Only when sensory input is presented |
| Olfactory | Only when sensory input is presented |

Table 4.4 provides a brief list of interventions that an OT might design for a child with ASD.

**Table 4.4**
**_Brief List of Sensory Interventions That an OT Might Prescribe for a Child with ASD_**

| Issue or Challenge | Possible Interventions |
|---|---|
| Has problems with sensory stimuli in lunchroom | ▪ Allow the child to go the cafeteria early.<br>▪ Allow the child to eat in the classroom or other nonstimulating environment.<br>▪ Decrease time in the lunchroom.<br>▪ Assist the child in setting up for the meal (opening milk, condiments, helping to select food). |
| Leans on table or desk | ▪ Provide opportunities for large-motor activities such as jumping, pulling, and pushing prior to these activities.<br>▪ Allow the child to stand during activities.<br>▪ Provide the child with legitimate opportunities to move, such as sharpening pencils or throwing away trash.<br>▪ Place rubberized shelf-lining or anti-slip material on the seat of the chair.<br>▪ Place a tennis ball on chair legs (diagonal). This allows for continual small movements. |

## Table 4.4 (cont.)

| | |
|---|---|
| Chews on pencils, pens, clothing | - Allow the child to chew on gum, gummy worms (chill to harden), jujubes, hard candy, coffee stirrers, latex-free tubing, straws, or give snacks that are crunchy or chewy.<br>- Allow the child to chew on clothes if it does not cause harm.<br>- Provide a water bottle with a sturdy straw that the child can drink from. |
| Has difficulty transitioning between activities | - Allow the child to be first or last in line.<br>- Allow the child to leave class five minutes early.<br>- Create a map that provides a visual plan or route between locations.<br>- Have the child hold the door open for the rest of the class by leaning her back into the door. This extra input may help tolerate the subsequent sensory input of the hall.<br>- Offer the child a signal before a change occurs, when possible.<br>- Provide deep-pressure activities that the child may utilize when a change occurs.<br>- Gradually incorporate "unplanned" activities into the schedule, starting with preferred activities.<br>- Incorporate a "change" symbol into the child's schedule. |
| Does not respond to name | - Teach the child to attend to his name by using games that involve saying his name and then reinforcing him for responding. For example, "Where is ____ ?" sung to the tune of "Where is Thumbkin?"<br>- Develop visual cues or signals to gain the child's attention.<br>- Vary your intonation or add melody, using a "sing-song" manner.<br>- Pair a novel auditory cue with name such as clicking fingers or clapping hands. |
| Talks self through task | - Allow the child to talk to self if it does not interfere with the functioning of others.<br>- Utilize a hand fidget to help decrease anxiety or enhance self-regulation.<br>- Provide a weighted lap pad for deep-pressure input.<br>- Develop visual supports that the child can use if in a situation where he is unable to talk himself through tasks without disturbing others. This might also give the extra support to refocus himself and continue if he becomes distracted for some reason.<br>- Teach the child to self-talk using a lower volume or stand away from others. |
| Has poor organization skills | - Provide visual structure through color-coding or special assignment books.<br>- Put tape inside the child's desk as a boundary marker for books.<br>- Organize materials under the desk or on a bookshelf so they are always visible.<br>- Use a sturdy box lid to contain student materials. Slide the box into the desk where it serves as a laptop desk.<br>- Provide a notebook to carry papers to and from home with clearly marked "Homework" sections for each subject. |

Adapted from *Asperger Syndrome and Sensory Issues: Practical Solutions for Making Sense of the World*, by B. S. Myles, K. T. Cook, N. E. Miller, L. Rinner, & L. Robbins, 2000, Shawnee Mission, KS: Autism Asperger Publishing Company. Reprinted with permission.

CAPS

# Summary

It is well documented that many individuals with ASD have significant sensory challenges. To prepare these students to learn and to support them while learning, sensory strategies can be an essential component in planning an effective daily schedule. The CAPS recognizes that for students who require sensory supports, such supports may be needed throughout the day. An OT trained in sensory integration, an essential member of the CAPS team, is a must when designing and implementing sensory supports.

# References

American Psychiatric Association. (2000). *Diagnostic and statistical manual for mental disorders* (4th ed., text revision). Washington, DC: Author.

Baranek, G. (2002). Efficacy of sensory and motor interventions for children with autism. *Journal of Autism and Developmental Disorders, 32*, 397-422.

Brack, J. C. (2004). *Learn to move, move to learn! Sensorimotor early childhood activity themes*. Shawnee Mission, KS: Autism Asperger Publishing Company.

Dunn, W., Myles, B. S., & Orr, S. (2002). Sensory processing issues associated with Asperger syndrome: A preliminary investigation. *The American Journal of Occupational Therapy, 56*(1), 97-102.

Gepner, B., & Mestre, D. R. (2002). Brief report: Postural reactivity to fast visual motion differentiates autistic from children with children with Asperger syndrome. *Journal of Autism and Developmental Disorders, 32*, 231-238.

Green, D., Baird, G., Barnett, A. L., Henderson, L., Huber, J., & Henderson, S. E. (2002). The severity and nature of motor impairment in Asperger's syndrome: A comparison with specific developmental disorder of motor function. *Journal of Child Psychology and Psychiatry, 43*, 655-668.

Kaplan, H., Clopton, M., Kaplan, M., Messbauer, L., & McPherson, K. (2006). Snoezelen multi-sensory environments: Task engagement and generalization. *Research in Developmental Disabilities, 27*, 443-455.

Myles, B. S., Hagiwara, T., Dunn, W., Rinner, L., Reese, M., Huggins, A., & Becker, S. (2004). Sensory issues in children with Asperger syndrome and autism. *Education and Training in Developmental Disabilities, 3*, 283-290.

Myles, B. S., Simpson, R. L., Carlson, J., Laurant, M., Gentry, A., Cook, K. T., & Earles-Vollrath, T. L. (2004). Examining the effects of the use of weighted vests for addressing behaviors of children with autism spectrum disorders. *Journal of the International Association of Special Educators, 5*(1), 47-62.

National Research Council. (Ed.). (2001). *Educating children with autism.* Washington, DC: National Academy Press.

Pfeiffer, B., Kinnealey, M., Reed, C., & Herzberg, G. (2005). Sensory modulation and affective disorders in children and adolescents with Asperger's disorder. *The American Journal of Occupational Therapy, 59*, 335-345.

Rogers, S. J., & Ozonoff, S. (2005). Annotation: What do we know about sensory dysfunction in autism? A critical review of the empirical evidence. *Journal of Child Psychology and Psychiatry, 46*, 1255-1268.

Schilling, D. L., & Schwartz, I. S. (2004). Alternative seating for young children with autism spectrum disorder" Effects on classroom behavior. *Journal of Autism and Developmental Disorders, 34*, 423-432.

# Communication/ Social Skills

*Teresa A. Cardon, M.A., CCC-SLP*

## CHAPTER 5

Communication and social interaction are two core areas that individuals with autism spectrum disorders (ASD) find challenging. According to the *Diagnostic and Statistical Manual of Mental Disorders* (4th Edition, Text Revision; DSM-IV, TR; American Psychiatric Association [APA], 2000), individuals with ASD exhibit qualitative impairments in communication and social interaction. While a communication impairment is often thought of as a lack of verbal speech, it may also be found in individuals with adequate verbal capabilities who struggle to initiate and sustain conversations with others.

To successfully communicate, a person must have a method to express himself, a partner to receive the communication, and the ability to comprehend the information that is communicated back to him. The communication

> To successfully communicate, a person must have a method to express himself, a partner to receive the communication, and the ability to comprehend the information that is communicated back to him.

73

of ideas, desires, or intentions is referred to as *expressive communication*. Expressive communication can refer to verbal and nonverbal acts. Understanding, or comprehending, communication, in turn, is defined as *receptive communication*. Finally, the set of social rules that govern the conversational use of language is known as *pragmatics*.

Keeping these three elements in mind, this chapter will focus on the struggles that some individuals with ASD experience with communication and social skills. It will also introduce a variety of strategies for use in individual and group instruction that may be beneficial to individuals with ASD and, therefore, need to be considered when completing a CAPS for a child.

# Communication

Individuals with ASD may have difficulties with several aspects of communication. For example, in the area of expressive communication, they may struggle to produce verbal speech. Some have difficulty initiating requests, either verbally or nonverbally, to a communication partner. Some may produce echolalic, or repeated, speech patterns that seem to have little or no meaning. Also, there are times when individuals with ASD struggle to know the underlying ideas or desires that they want to express. These examples are in no way inclusive or exhaustive, but they represent some of the specific areas that can make expressive communication difficult.

Receptive communication is also problematic for many on the autism spectrum. Students may have problems understanding verbal input and, despite responding to adult queries, often have little idea what was said to them. Instead they process and respond with greater accuracy to visually presented information.

# Role of Motivation

One of the most basic reasons why children first learn to communicate is to get their needs met. They decide they need or want something, and then through verbal (crying, talking, etc.) or nonverbal (pushing, pulling, pointing, etc.) means they go about expressing themselves. During these early exchanges, a child's motivation to achieve a desired result is a key factor. Motivation has also been found to be a pivotal element when individuals with ASD are discovering pathways to expressive communication. That is, when a child is motivated, her ability to participate and stay involved in an activity increases. Research suggests that children with autism initiate more for items or activities that are motivating (Koegel & Koegel, 2006).

> Research suggests that children with autism initiate more for items or activities that are motivating (Koegel & Koegel, 2006).

# Initiations

Helping children learn to initiate is another pivotal skill when it comes to effective expressive communication. There are many different types of initiations. Children initiate to request something, to gain someone's attention, or to ask a question, but what exactly does initiation mean?

An initiation is an independently created communicative act. Initiation is a more challenging than responding because children have to create their own independent thoughts and ideas and are not able to get ideas from or build on someone else's questions or comments. A child who can initiate will be able to get others to respond to him and in turn improve his overall communication and language skills (Koegel & Koegel, 2006).

Initiations are broken down into three categories: behavior regulation, social communication, and joint attention. When children initiate for *behavior regulation,* it is to get their basic needs met – requests for food, drink, comfort, etc. Initiations for *social communication* are about two people interacting. At this level, children initiate to ask questions, take turns, gain information and relate with another person. Finally, at the *joint attention* level, children initiate to simultaneously attend with another person to an event or an object. In other words, they initiate to share a single focus. Initiating for joint attention can happen verbally or nonverbally but always involves the ability to think about another person's thoughts and ideas. Teaching individuals with ASD to initiate is vital to successful social communication.

## Interventions

***Picture Exchange Communication System.*** The Picture Exchange Communication System (PECS) is an alternative form of communication that teaches individuals to use pictures to express themselves. PECS is a research-based strategy (Frost & Bondy, 2002) that is based on the principles of applied behavior analysis.

Some parents and professionals worry that if a child is encouraged to use pictures to communicate, she will shy away from verbal speech. In reality, the research on PECS (cf., Charlop-Christy, Carpenter, Le, LeBlanc, & Kellet, 2002; Jones, 2005; Magiati & Howlin, 2003; Tien, in press) indicates that many children develop verbal speech when they are introduced to PECS, particularly when the number of pictures that they use increases.

Parents and researchers have also noted a decrease in a child's disruptive or inappropriate behaviors when PECS was used (Anderson, 2002; Charlop-Christy et al., 2002; Magiati & Howlin, 2003). For example, if a child is hungry, she may cry to indicate that she is hungry. A teacher or parent may not know that the child is crying to express hunger and, as a result, the child's needs remain unmet.

By contrast, a child who is taught to exchange a picture of a food item when hungry will get the food he wants and remain regulated throughout the exchange, thereby decreasing the levels of

> The Picture Exchange Communication System (PECS) is an alternative form of communication that teaches individuals to use pictures to express themselves.

frustration he may have been previously displaying.

**Sign language.** While there is no clear research on which communication system works best for a specific individual with ASD, some

---

*Note.* It is important to note that PECS does not mean "pictures" but is a specific strategy for teaching children to exchange pictures as a way of communicating. One key component of PECS is that children learn to initiate their needs and wants through the use of pictures. In order for PECS to be effective, it is important to determine a child's key motivators, or reinforcers.

have found success with sign language (Goldstein, 2002). Several videos, such as *Baby Signs* (Acredolo & Goodwyn, 2002), were created to specifically teach young children to sign. It is important when teaching sign language that specific labels for objects are taught, not just generic terms (i.e., "more" or "eat"). In that way, the child can directly tell a communication partner *what* he wants more of or *what* he wants to eat.

Individuals who use sign language must also be taught to show, or direct, their sign to another person. Without knowing that the sign must be directed to another person, the individual signing will not be able to get his needs met. Finally, it is important that siblings and peers be partners in communication and can understand and use sign language with the individual with ASD to further support social interactions. Therefore, they also need to learn at least some basic signs.

***Pivotal Response Training.*** Pivotal Response Training (PRT) is an empirically based intervention that includes using motivational procedures and natural reinforcers in natural environments (Koegel & Koegel, 2006). Research on PRT indicates that if certain pivotal skills are taught to a child, learning those pivotal skills will affect other areas of a child's development (Baker-Ericzen, Stahmer, & Burns, 2007; Pierce & Schreibman, 1995, 1997; Sherer & Schreibman, 2005; Stahmer, 1995). The four pivotal areas that have been researched by the Koegels include (a) motivation, (b) multiple cues, (c) self-initiation, and (d) self-management.

PRT has been successfully used to teach some children with autism to use verbal communication. The critical features in teaching children to verbalize using PRT include intensity and consistency of the intervention, family involvement, a functional approach to problem behaviors, and motivation. The steps to implementing PRT may be found in Table 5.1.

### Table 5.1
### *Steps to Implementing PRT*

| PRT Element | Description |
|---|---|
| Natural environment and caregivers | The environment should be arranged to increase a child's opportunities for communication. Caregivers should be a part of the intervention. |
| Motivation | Child choice should start the interaction. A child must be motivated enough to continue trying to get the object or activity. Talking is not easy, and the child must be willing to persist. |
| Instruction and response | Instruction should be delivered clearly while the child is attending to the task. The child's response should be clear, directed, and appropriate to the task. |
| Maintenance tasks | Novel, difficult tasks should be interspersed with familiar, successful activities so the child does not get frustrated. |
| Contingency | **If** the child produces a vocalization, **then** the child gets the object or activity. |
| Reinforcement of attempts | Reasonable attempts should IMMEDIATELY be reinforced. A reasonable attempt initially is any sound that is directed and related to the task. |
| Direct and natural reinforcers | Reinforcement should be directly and functionally related. For example, if a child is interested in a ball, share control of the ball and use it as the direct and natural reinforcer. When the child vocalizes a reasonable attempt, reinforce the child with the ball. |

Using PRT to encourage verbal language and first words creates multiple opportunities throughout the day for a child to practice because the intervention takes place in a natural environment using natural reinforcers.

***Assistive technology.*** The Individuals with Disabilities Education Act (IDEA) and the Technology-Related Assistance for Individuals Act

(TRAIDA; 1988) define assistive technology as "any item, piece of equipment, or product system, whether acquired commercially off the shelf, modified, or customized, that is used to increase, maintain, or improve functional capabilities of individuals with disabilities."

Assistive technology is often referred to as low-tech, meaning simplistic and limited in function, or high-tech, characterized as multifunctional and complex (Langone, Malone, & Kinsley, 1999). Low-tech options include items such as pictures, Velcro™ straps, rubber mats, photographs, adaptive spoons, and so on, whereas high-tech devices include computerized or augmentative communication devices with voice output capabilities and similar products. PECS is a type of low-tech assistive technology that can support communication in individuals with ASD.

Using high-tech computerized devices, children learn to press on pictures, and the voice output on the device states what they would like to say (Millar, Light, & Schlosser, 2006). Families and school districts require support and training to program and utilize high-tech devices effectively. Unfortunately, there are a limited number of trained professionals available to support individuals and families using high-tech devices; in fact, the most common reason families abandon AT is a lack of training (Parette, VanBiervliet, & Hourcade, 2000).

***Natural Aided Language System.*** The Natural Aided Language System (NALS; Cafiero, 2001) is a classroom-based augmentative communication intervention that pairs spoken verbal language with visual supports in a variety of natural contexts throughout the day.

As opposed to following a more linear language development strategy targeting first nouns or object labels, NALS introduces multiple communication functions, such as initiating, asking questions, responding, and commenting in a more spontaneous and holistic fashion.

Pictures, or visual symbols, of contextually appropriate vocabulary are organized on specific language boards to support a specific environment in the classroom. Language boards include various parts of speech such as nouns, verbs, and adjectives to increase the communication functions available to the teachers and students. For example, a language board for snack time may include pictures to represent the words *I, you, do, want, can, have, am, juice, cookie, cracker, water, yes, no, all done*. The teacher would use the language board paired with her spoken language to ask the question, "Do you want juice?" The child responds by touching pictures to indicate "yes" or ask for something other than juice; for example, "I want water."

Teachers use the language boards to model the child's intended request, even if the child does not use the language board symbols. Children are exposed to the paired systems of verbal and visual language throughout the day in multiple contexts to increase their expressive and receptive language skills. A sample NALS appears in Figure 5.1.

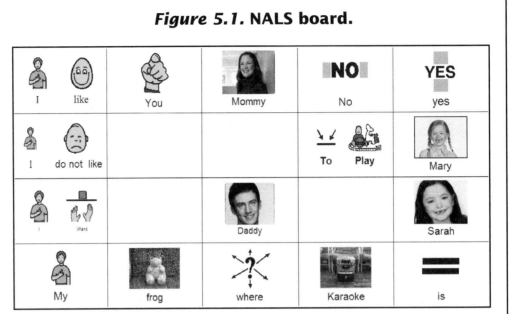

**Figure 5.1. NALS board.**

# Self-Awareness

Self-awareness, often a deficit area for individuals with ASD, also involves communication – personal communication about what is occurring in the environment, how it impacts the individual and what, if any, action should be taken. Persons with ASD experience varying degrees of ability to understand their own feelings. As a result, they do not detect how they feel and hence do not know when to self-calm, for example. This is compounded by the challenges many individuals with ASD experience in understanding what self-calming strategies are available and how to use them (Barnhill, 2001; Barnhill et al., 2000).

It is important to ensure that individuals with ASD have opportunities to learn more about their actions and behaviors to help them develop self-awareness in different situations and environments. For example, many struggle to regulate their behaviors when they become angry or upset, not because they are inconsiderate of others, but because they do not have an innate understanding that it is important to be considerate of others. Several instructional strategies have been created specifically to target self-awareness in individuals with ASD.

## Interventions

***Stress Thermometer.*** As mentioned in Chapter 4, individuals with ASD may have a difficult time processing sensory information, which can lead to difficulties with emotional regulation. A Stress Thermometer (see Figure 5.2) (McAfee, 2002) is a visual tool that can support individuals in identifying their bodies' "stress signals;" that is, their physical reactions to stressful situations. In addition to listing stress signals, the thermometer also lists relaxation techniques and suggestions, making specific strategies readily available.

For example, a Stress Thermometer might state "humming loudly and tapping my pencil" to describe a child's physical reactions to stress. An accompanying relaxation suggestion could be "play with a fidget toy and take a short break." When creating a Stress Thermometer, it is helpful to provide the child support in tracking his stressful moments on a special Stress Tracking Chart (see Figure 5.3) (McAfee, 2002). Stress tracking charts allow for specific stressful times of day, locations, and triggering events to be mapped out and documented.

Finally, based on the findings of the Stress Tracking Sheet, a Summary of Stress Signals (see Figure 5.4) (McAfee, 2002) worksheet can be created to specify what clues the individual with ASD may provide, either verbally or physically, to indicate the stress level she is experiencing. Helping an individual on the spectrum recognize symptoms of personal stress and the level of that stress goes a long way in promoting self awareness skills. Figures 5.2, 5.3, and 5.4 provide examples of worksheets designed by McAfee (2002) for a student she refers to as Scott W.

### Figure 5.2. Stress thermometer.

## Stress Thermometer

**For:** Scott W.

**Stress signals:**

teeth & fists clenched
squints
talks loud & fast
paces

hums
plays with hair
glares at other people
taps fingers on desk

hunched-over posture
quieter than usual
glazed expression
high-pitched voice

10
9
8
7
6
5
4
3
2
1

**Stress signals:**

*High stress*

swing
"walk, no talk"
break time – go to quiet place

*Moderate stress*

listen to relaxing music
use Thera-putty
break time – go to quiet place

*Low stress*

visualize being at beach
close eyes, put head down on desk
roll shoulders & neck

From *Navigating the Social World: A Curriculum for Individuals with Asperger's Syndrome, High Functioning Autism and Related Disorders* (p. 47) by J. McAfee, 2002. Copyright 2002 by Future Horizons, Inc. Reprinted with permission.

## Figure 5.3. Stress tracking sheet.

**Home/School**     **Stress Tracking Sheet**     **Student:** Scott W.

| Date & Time | Precipitating event (trigger) | Underlying or "hidden" stressor(s) and related emotions | *Stress Signals* Body language, facial expressions & verbal cues (as observed) | Physical symptoms (by student report) | Stress level: Low, Moderate, High | Outcome |
|---|---|---|---|---|---|---|
| 4/1/00 9:30 am | Ian sat in Scott's usual chair during art class | Anxiety due to schedule changes that week | Playing with hair Humming | Not obtainable | Moderate | Shoved Ian <br> ▪ Sent to principal |
| 4/2/00 10:10 am | Joe borrowed Scott's pencil and then lost it | Angry because he was teased on the school bus that morning | Jaws and teeth clenched Squinting | Muscles tense Increased heart rate | High | Shouted swear word Threw paperwork on floor ▪ Sent to principal |
| 4/5/00 2:30 pm | Scott didn't finish math problems before class ended | Frustrated, unable to concentrate due to noise from photocopy machine in next room | Humming Tapping on desk Playing with hair | Headache Stomach ache | Moderate | Shouted at teacher that he "had to finish" ▪ Points taken off math grade |
| 4/6/00 1:30 pm | Bill accidentally bumped into Scott on playground at lunch | On playground for entire lunchtime. Difficulty joining in with other kids. Frustrated, lonely | Humming Glaring | Not obtainable | Moderate | Yelled at Bill and complained to playground aid ▪ No further consequences |
| 4/7/00 10:05 am | Teacher gently corrected Scott's verbal answer in class | Some other students had giggled last period when Scott was reading report in front of class | Teeth & fists clenched Squinting Talking loud and fast | Face hot Muscles tense Stomach ache | High | Fumed out of room yelling. "I don't like any of you" ▪ Discussion with teacher |
| 4/8/00 3:15 pm | Joe slapped Scott on the back as a nice "hello" in hall | Group art project in afternoon | Hunched over | Headache Muscles tense Stomach ache | Low | Scowled at other student ▪ No further consequences |
| 4/9/00 12:30 pm | Working on grammar assignment | Photocopy machine in next room | Glazed expression Quiet | Shoulder muscles tense Mild headache | Low | Unable to focus on work |

From *Navigating the Social World: A Curriculum for Individuals with Asperger's Syndrome, High Functioning Autism and Related Disorders* by J. McAfee (p. 29, 30), 2002. Copyright 2002 by Future Horizons, Inc. Reprinted with permission.

**Figure 5.4.** Summary of stress signals.

**Summary of Stress Signals**

Student: <u>Scott W.</u>

| | Low stress | Moderate stress | High stress |
|---|---|---|---|
| **Verbal & nonverbal clues**<br><br><br>Body language, facial expressions & verbal clues<br><br>(As observed by others. Data from Stress Tracking Charts) | Hunched-over Quiet, high-pitched voice<br><br>Glazed expression | Humming<br><br>Playing with hair<br><br>Glares<br><br>Tapping fingers on desk | Teeth clenched<br><br>Fists clenched<br><br>Squinting<br><br>Talks loud & fast<br><br>Pacing |
| ***Physical symptoms***<br><br><br>(As reported by student. Data from Stress Tracking Charts) | Shoulder muscles tense<br><br>Mild headache | Muscles tense generally<br><br>Stomachache<br><br>Headache | Muscles very tense<br><br>Stomachache<br><br>Sweaty palms<br><br>Breathing very fast<br><br>Increased heart rate<br><br>Face hot |

***The Incredible 5-point scale.*** Created by Buron and Curtis (2003), *The Incredible 5-Point Scale* is a self-awareness tool with a wide range of applications. Briefly, the individual with ASD describes the five different points on the scale in his own words. He then describes what each behavior feels like at that particular number. Finally, often with adult input, he describes the actions that need to be taken (by himself or by an adult) to address the behavior.

For example, if a child struggles to use his "inside voice" in the classroom, a 5-point scale may be created to give a number rank to different levels of loudness. A 5 may be yelling, a 3 may be talking inside, and a 1 may represent a whisper. This way the child gets a visual picture of what an inside voice sounds like. The flexibility of the scale allows it to be used with a variety of behaviors, from running in the hall to pulling a seat partner's hair during a test.

Figure 5.5 provides a sample Incredible 5-Point Scale for Joey, a third-grade student with Asperger Syndrome who often yelled at students who said things that bothered him. He did not realize that words could be hurtful because they did not cause bodily harm. This figure also includes a cartoon that helped Joey understand his behavior and a story that clarifies how words can hurt others.

## Figure 5.5. Joey's touching and talking 5-point scale.

From *The Incredible 5-Point Scale*, by K. D. Buron & M. Curtis, 2003 (pp. 10, 11, 12). Shawnee Mission, KS: Autism Asperger Publishing Company. Reprinted with permission.

***Self-calming routines.*** Because anxiety is a well-documented concern for many children with ASD (Barnhill et al., 2000; Bellini, 2006), it is essential that they be taught self-calming skills.

One of the keys to self-calming is that the person's high-anxiety stressors along with relaxation techniques are discussed before a state of disregulation is reached. *When My Worries Get Too Big!* for younger children (Buron, 2006) and *A 5 Is Against the Law! Social Boundaries Straight Up! An Honest Guide for Teens and Young Adults* for older children (Buron, 2007) are two tools that can help students become more self-aware and, therefore, better able to regulate their behaviors.

Specific situations and daily activities that can cause high anxiety are discussed with an adult at a time when the student is calm, along with corresponding relaxation techniques. For example, if a child finds assemblies in the multipurpose room to be overwhelming, specific strategies such as ear plugs, entering the room early before the noise is already at its peak, sitting near an exit, etc., can be discussed ahead of time so that the child has a clear plan to implement when anxiety may be heightened. An activity from Buron's (2007) *A 5 Is Against the Law!* appears in Figure 5.6.

**Figure 5.6.** Ideas for keeping calm.

# Ideas for Keeping Your Body Calm or for Pulling Yourself down from a 4 to a 2, or from a 3 to a 1

- **Try organized relaxation classes at least two times a week.** This can be done as a part of your school program, at home or at a YMCA. The idea is to learn ways to help your body stay at a lower level all the time. Yoga and some of the martial arts are perfect ideas for this.

- **Learn about breathing.** Breathing can become very shallow when we are upset, and this makes it harder to calm down. When you are feeling upset, *slow your breathing down*. Take deep breaths and think about pulling the air from your feet all the way up and out the top of your head.

- **Put a small photo album together with pictures of things that make you feel good and calm.** Keep the photo album in your desk, in your purse or in a briefcase. If you are having a rough day, find a quiet place to sit and look at the photos. If you have a favorite place like a summer cabin, a boat or even a back yard swing, take a picture of it and put it in your photo album. When you look at the picture of a favorite place, close your eyes and think about being there.

- **Try a calming sequence.** A calming sequence is a short series of relaxing actions that you can practice many times throughout the day. If you do this routine enough, you will be able to use it in a crisis to help you calm your body and your brain.

- **Listen to calming music.** There are many kinds of music designed to relax and calm listeners such as nature sounds.

***Asperger Syndrome: An Owner's Manual.*** The interactive workbook *Asperger Syndrome: An Owner's Manual* (Korin, 2006) is specifically designed to promote self-awareness in individuals with AS, grades five through eight. The book provides basic information on AS and different ways that individuals with AS function. It also provides opportunities for children to write down specific information about themselves, such as strengths, weaknesses, likes, dislikes, what works, what does not, and so on, as a means of making themselves more aware and communicating this information to parents and teachers.

As shown in Figure 5.7, the *Owner's Manual* operates as a type of road map for an individual child and is an effective tool on the path to self-awareness.

***How Does My Engine Run?*** Another strategy that promotes self-awareness is The Alert Program (Williams & Shellenberger, 1996), which uses the analogy of a car engine to represent the human body. Just like a car engine, sometimes a child's body runs high, sometimes it runs low, and at other times it seems to be running "just right." The specific stages and mile markers laid out in the program encourage children to identify how their own engine runs so that they can find support to regulate their engine, or body, thereby promoting the optimum level for learning and actively participating in the educational environment.

For example, if a child recognizes and reports that her engine is running high as the class is about to take a test, a teacher or other adult can help the child slow her engine down through a series of relaxation techniques or other calming activities relevant to the specific child so that she becomes more regulated and is able to take the test.

## *Figure 5.7.* Summary of personal profile.

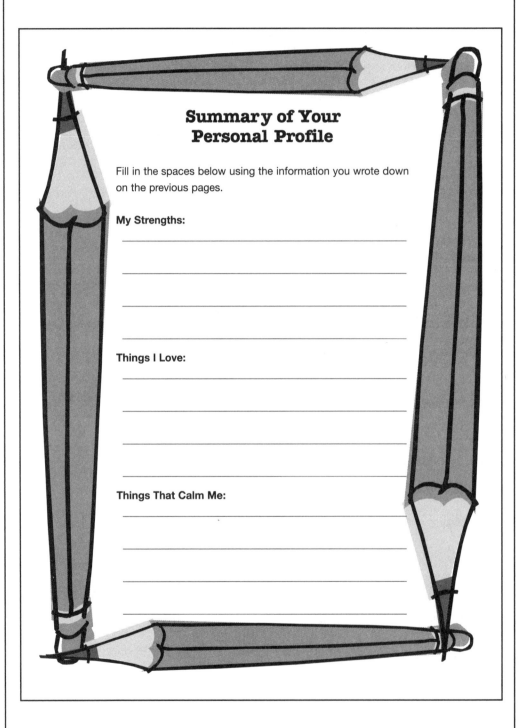

**Summary of Your
Personal Profile**

Fill in the spaces below using the information you wrote down on the previous pages.

**My Strengths:**

_____
_____
_____
_____

**Things I Love:**

_____
_____
_____
_____

**Things That Calm Me:**

_____
_____
_____
_____

From *Asperger Syndrome: An Owner's Manual*, by E. Korin, 2006 (p. 11). Shawnee Mission, KS: Autism Asperger Publishing Company. Reprinted with permission.

# Social Skills

Because a marked impairment in social interaction is one of the core features of ASD, it is imperative that comprehensive autism planning incorporate social skills instruction for every child. It is important to note, however, that all individuals with ASD do not exhibit social skills deficits in a uniform manner. As a result, social skills instruction must be individualized to meet the needs of every child. While limited in terms of a research base, a growing number of social skills tools have been shown to be effective with a variety of individuals in many different settings.

# Interventions

*Social Stories™* (Gray, 2000). Social Stories™ are meant to provide individuals with the information they need to make sound decisions about a variety of situations. Social Stories™ also provide a unique opportunity to look at the different perspectives people may take when experiencing the same situation.

Briefly, Social Stories™ take a social encounter and break it down in manageable parts that can be explained and sorted in detail. Many individuals with ASD have found this intervention to be a practical, no-nonsense guide to challenging social scenarios. Social Stories™ (see Gray, 2000) may be written for specific situations. This feature makes them a great option and very personalized to an individual's strengths and/or weaknesses.

***Social Scripts.*** The idea behind social scripts is to give a child direct language to use in a particular social scenario. If a child with ASD has difficulty joining a group of children at recess, for example, the script can describe the situation and offer specific phrases that the child could use to join the group. The script should be written from the point of view of the child so that it is grammatically appropriate. During the recess scenario the script may read, "Can I play with you?"

It is important to practice the script with the child and incorporate scenarios that could occur once the child has used the scripted language. For example, individuals with ASD need to be aware of possible reactions their peers could have so that they are not caught off guard and left feeling unsuccessful and frustrated. For example, what if the peers say "No"? The child with ASD needs to know how to successfully leave the group and not continue trying to join in. Practicing the script with supportive peers in a safe environment is a good place to start.

***Power Cards*** (Gagnon, 2001). Power Cards are similar to Social Stories™ and social scripts, but they add a unique twist by incorporating an individual's special interest as a motivating factor to increase his or her understanding in social situations. Parents and professionals can script out the social scenario that the child is struggling with. The script should be written at the appropriate comprehension level for the child and should include how the child's special interest character or hero managed to find a successful solution.

Once the script is finished, a Power Card, a small business card or 3x5 card, may be created to highlight the key steps and strategies that are necessary for successful participation in the social routine being addressed. A sample Power Card scenario and accompanying Power Card appears in Figure 5.8.

---

### *Figure 5.8.* **Sample power card scenario.**

The power card, scenario and background information on Wilbur Takes Charge from the special interest on Charlotte's Web in Elisa's book.

---

#### *Greg*

Greg is an 11-year-old boy with autism. He is prompt-dependent throughout the school day, looking to his teacher or paraprofessionals to provide him with every instruction. Greg is interested in cartoon videos and his parents report that his favorite video is *Charlotte's Web*. The following scenario and POWER CARD were developed to address Greg's prompt dependency.

#### *Wilbur Takes Charge*
##### by Cindy Van Horn

*Charlotte the spider loves her best friend, Wilbur the pig. Lately, Charlotte has been frustrated with Wilbur because he will not do anything unless she tells him what to do. Wilbur will not eat unless Charlotte tells him it is time to eat. Wilbur will not clean his pigpen unless Charlotte tells him to clean it. In fact, Wilbur won't even play with the other pigs unless Charlotte tells him it's time to play. Charlotte is tired! She knows Wilbur will be a happier pig if he asks for help instead of always having to be told what to do.*

---

*Just like Wilbur, it is important for all boys at school to be independent. It is important to do your work on your own without someone telling you what to do. If you don't know what to do, it is OK to ask for help. For example, boys can go through the lunch line by themselves without someone telling them every step they need to take. Of course, boys can always ask for help if they need it. Charlotte has decided she is going to wait for Wilbur to ask for help instead of always telling him what to do. She wants Wilbur to take charge!*

1. If you are not sure what to do, check your schedule.
2. Don't wait for someone to tell you what to do. Just do it!!
3. If you need help say, "I need help."

*Just remember Charlotte's three rules for taking charge:*

*1. If you are not sure what to do, check your schedule.*

*2. Don't wait for someone to tell you what to do. Just do it!!*

*3. If you need help say, "I need help."*

*Remember these three things and you can take charge just like Wilbur!*

---

From *Power Cards: Using Special Interests to Motivate Children and Youth With Asperger Syndrome and Autism*, by E. Gagnon (pp. 48 & 49). Shawnee Mission, KS: Autism Asperger Publishing Company. Reprinted with permission.

***Conversation starters.*** These are similar to Power Cards in that they are small business cards or 3x5 cards that individuals with ASD can keep on hand; however, they differ in terms of their function. Designed to help begin conversations with peers, the cards list several topics that would be considered "current" and appropriate for a particular peer group.

For example, if a group of 9-year-old girls at school often talk about their collections of The Littlest Pet Shop characters, then a topic appropriate for a conversation starter card would be Littlest Pet Shop. The card could state things like, "Do you have any Littlest Pet Shop figures?" or "What is your favorite Littlest Pet Shop figure?"

It is important to determine what the most appropriate conversation starters are based on the group of peers that the individual with ASD is most likely to join. Every school has its own culture – what might be considered popular at one school may not be at another.

***Special interests.*** Using special interests is another great way for children with ASD to practice interacting socially with peers. When individuals with ASD are allowed to discuss and explore their special interests in an environment created specifically for those special interests, their desire to interact and socialize can increase. If a child loves airplanes, create an airplane club. If a child really loves comic books, invite peers to join a comic book club. Chances are that other students will be interested in the topic, too. These clubs can provide structured opportunities for individuals with ASD to practice the social skills they are working on.

# Summary

Communication strategies must be integrated into the student's day in order to make instruction meaningful. Strategies that focus on being functional and practical and support communication in all environments with family members, peers, and the entire community are the type of supports that should be a part of a student's CAPS.

# References

Acredolo, L., & Goodwyn, S. (2002). *Baby signs: How to talk with your baby before your baby can talk.* Columbus, OH: McGraw-Hill.

American Psychiatric Association. (2000). *Diagnostic and statistical manual for mental disorders* (4th ed., text revision). Washington, DC: Author.

Anderson, A. E. (2002). Augmentative communication and autism: A comparison of sign language and the Picture Exchange Communication System (Doctoral dissertation, University of California, San Diego, 2001). *Dissertation Abstracts International, 62*(9-B), 4269.

Baker-Ericzen, M. J., Stahmer, A. C., & Burns, A. (2007). Child demographics associated with outcomes in a community-based pivotal response training program. *Journal of Positive Behavior Interventions, 9*, 52-59.

Barnhill, G. P. (2001). Social attribution and depression in adolescents with Asperger syndrome. *Focus on Autism and Other Developmental Disabilities, 16*, 46-53.

Barnhill, G. P., Hagiwara, T., Myles, B. S., Simpson, R. L., Brick, M. L., & Griswold, D. E. (2000). Parent, teacher, and self-report of problem and adaptive behaviors in children and adolescents with Asperger syndrome. *Diagnostique, 25*(2), 147-167.

Bellini, S. (2006). The development of social anxiety in adolescents with autism spectrum disorders. *Focus on Autism and Other Developmental Disabilities, 21,* 138-145.

Buron, K. (2006). *When my worries get too big! A relaxation book for children with autism spectrum disorders.* Shawnee Mission, KS: Autism Asperger Publishing Company.

Buron, K. (2007). *A "5" could make me lose control.* Shawnee Mission, KS: Autism Asperger Publishing Company.

Buron, K. (2007). *A 5 is against the law!* Shawnee Mission, KS: Autism Asperger Publishing Company.

Buron, K., & Curtis, M. (2003). *The incredible 5-point scale: Assisting students with autism spectrum disorders in understanding social interactions and controlling their emotions.* Shawnee Mission, KS: Autism Asperger Publishing Company.

Cafiero, J. M. (2001). The effect of an augmentative communication intervention on the communication, behavior, and academic program of an adolescent with autism. *Focus on Autism and Other Developmental Disabilities, 16,* 179-189.

Charlop-Christy, M., Carpenter, M., Le, L., LeBlanc, L., & Kellet, K. (2002). Using the Picture Exchange Communication System (PECS) with children with autism: Assessment of PECS acquisition, speech, social communicative behavior, and problem behavior. *Journal of Applied Behavior Analysis, 35,* 213-231.

Frost, L., & Bondy, A. (2002). *The Picture Exchange Communication System training manual.* Newark, DE: Pyramid Educational Products.

Gagnon, E. (2001). *Power Cards: Using special interests to motivate children and youth with Asperger Syndrome and autism.* Shawnee Mission, KS: Autism Asperger Publishing Company.

Goldstein, H. (2002). Communication intervention for children with autism: A review of treatment efficacy. *Journal of Autism and Developmental Disorders, 32,* 373-396.

Gray, C. (2000). *Writing social stories with Carol Gray.* Arlington, TX: Future Horizons.

Jones, C. M. (2005). Using Picture Exchange Communication System and time delay to enhance the spontaneous speech of children with autism (Doctoral dissertation, Claremont Graduation University, 2004). *Dissertation Abstracts International, 65*(8-B), 4270.

Koegel, L., & Koegel, R. (2006). *Pivotal response treatments for autism.* Baltimore: Paul H. Brookes.

Korin, E. (2006). *Asperger Syndrome: An owner's manual.* Shawnee Mission, KS: Autism Asperger Publishing Company.

Langone, J., Malone, D. M., & Kinsley, T. (1999). Technology solutions for young children with developmental concerns. *Infants and Young Children, 11,* 65-78.

Magiati, I., & Howlin, P. (2003). A pilot evaluation study of the Picture Exchange Communication System for children with Autistic Spectrum Disorder. *Autism: The International Journal of Research and Practice, 7,* 297-320.

McAfee, J. (2002). *Navigating the social world: A curriculum for individuals with Asperger syndrome, high functioning autism, and related disorders.* Arlington, TX: Future Horizons.

Millar, D., Light, J., & Schlosser, R. (2006). The impact of augmentative and alternative communication intervention on the speech production of individuals with developmental disabilities: A research review. *Journal of Speech, Language & Hearing Research, 49,* 248-264.

Parette, H. P., VanBiervliet, A., & Hourcade, J. J. (2000). Family-centered decision-making in assistive technology. *Journal of Special Education Technology, 15*(1), 45-55.

Pierce, K., & Schreibman, L. (1995). Multiple peer use of pivotal response training to increase social behaviors of classmates with autism: Results from trained and untrained peers. *Journal of Applied Behavior Analysis, 30,* 157-164.

Pierce, K., & Schreibman, L. (1997). Increasing complex social behaviors in children with autism: Effects of peer-implemented pivotal response training. *Journal of Applied Behavior Analysis, 28,* 285-311.

Sherer, M. R., & Schreibman, L. (2005). Individual behavioral profiles and predictors of treatment effectiveness for children with autism. *Journal of Consulting and Clinical Psychology, 73*, 525-539.

Stahmer, A. C. (1995). Teaching symbolic play skills to children with autism using pivotal response training. *Journal of Autism and Developmental Disorders, 25*, 123-141.

*Technology-Related Assistance for Individuals with Disabilities Act of 1988.* Public Law 100-406.

Tien, K. (in press). Effectiveness of the Picture Exchange Communication System as a functional communication intervention for individuals with autism spectrum disorders: A practice-based research synthesis. *Education and Training in Developmental Disabilities.*

Williams, M. S., & Shellenberger, S. (1996). *How does your engine run? A leader's guide to the alert program for self-regulation.* Albuquerque, NM: TherapyWorks.

# Data Collection

*Andi Babkie, Ph.D.*

## CHAPTER 6

One of the basics of the CAPS process – as is true of special education programming in general – is to have clearly defined IEP (individualized education program) goals and objectives that are readily accessible to all involved in working with the student. A next step is taking those goals and objectives, matching them with an intervention, and then determining both the efficacy of the intervention and the appropriateness of the goals and objectives.

This is where collecting data comes in. Based on what is discovered in the data, interventions may be altered or may be continued as is; objectives may be adjusted if it is found that they have been mastered or that they are inappropriate at the moment; and changes may occur in the process of encouraging generalization through increasing a student's self-monitoring. Whatever the case may be, the collection and sharing of data is vital to increasing success for students.

Data collection involves gathering information about how an individual is performing in terms of a specific social or academic behavior. This information is then used both to measure progress and to make decisions. To gain accurate information, the process must be systematic and ongoing. This chapter describes how to determine the behavior(s) to select, the methods for collecting data, and the overall procedures for effective use of the data collected.

# The Data Collection Process

Data collection is a multistep process that begins with selecting the target behavior and ends with using the collected information in making decisions. This also includes deciding the who, what, where, when, why, and how of the process to achieve success for the student. The steps of this process are as follows:

1. Establishing the target behavior

2. Deciding on a system for collecting the data

3. Determining when and where data will be collected

4. Determining who will collect the data

5. Determining a system for sharing data

6. Using information collected for decision making

*Establishing the target behavior.* The first step in collecting data is to establish the targeted behavior. While the student's IEP includes goals and objectives, the target behaviors are generally more discrete behaviors, representing a step on the way toward achieving the objective. For example, if a social objective for a student is to "interact with peers," a target behavior for the student might be to "respond when greeted by a peer." Data would then be collected on this specific target behavior rather than on the objective as a whole. Once that target behavior had been mastered, another behavior in the sequence to achieve the objective is selected and measured.

Once the target behavior is selected, it is important to make sure it is described in terms that are specific, objective, and measurable. Figure 6.1 provides an overview of what does and does not describe a good target behavior.

---

### *Figure 6.1.* Targeted behaviors: What they are and what they are not.

A targeted behavior must be:

- **Specific:** It is clear enough so that two independent observers would count the same number of instances of behavior. You can define it.

- **Observable:** You can see it.

- **Measurable:** You can count it in some fashion.

- **Voluntary:** It may be changed.

- **Replicable:** It may be done again.

| Non-Example: | Example: |
|---|---|
| Be annoying | Touch others |
| | Take others' possessions |
| Act appropriately | Raise hand |
| | Wait in line until called |

---

**Deciding on a system for collecting the data.** Once the target behavior has been identified and defined, the next step is to select a system for data collection that matches the behavior. Observational data recording systems allow for observation and recording of behavior as it occurs in the classroom and are particularly useful in analyzing questions such as those that address student response to instruction, student engagement, and student behaviors. Many other systems are also available, as illustrated in Figure 6.2.

---

### *Figure 6.2.* Commonly used observational data recording systems.

- **Event Recording** – an exact measure of behavior

  ◆ use for discrete behaviors (those that have a definite beginning and end)

  ◆ count/tally how many times behavior occurs

    - Examples: raise hand, call out, ask question

- **Latency Recording** – an exact measure of behavior

  ◆ measure how long it takes to begin something

    - Examples: follow directions, begin work

- **Duration Recording** – an exact measure of behavior

  ◆ measure how long a behavior persists

    - Examples: temper tantrum, out of seat

- **Time Sampling** – an estimate of behaviors

  ◆ use for ongoing or high-frequency behaviors

  ◆ record whether behavior is or is not occurring at the end of every specific period of time (for example, every 30 seconds) for a specific session (for example, a session of 5 minutes at the beginning of class)

    - Examples: talk to peers (if high frequency), stay on task

---

The decision about which data collection method to use depends on the type of behavior that is being targeted, including its frequency and intensity. For example, a low-incidence behavior with a definite beginning and end (such as "open book") may best be measured by event recording because it is easily counted. On the other hand, an ongoing or high-frequency behavior (such as a self-stimulatory behavior) may best be measured through use of time sampling. When working with high-frequency or ongoing behaviors, it is difficult to count each instance of the behavior. Therefore, checking periodically (time sampling) to see if these behaviors are being displayed gives a fairly accurate picture of the behavior and prevents the data collection process from becoming overwhelming.

# Keeping Track of Data

Once a decision has been made about the method of data collection, the next decision involves how to keep track of the data collected to make it easy to analyze. This may come in the form of a data collection sheet or some other means. For observational recording systems, educators may design their own data collection sheets (see Figures 6.3 through 6.8) or select one from a number of commercially packaged products (e.g., Sprick & Howard, 1995). Each data collection system is specified in more detail below.

*Event recording* gives an exact measure of behavior because each instance is counted. Therefore, as noted above, it is used for behaviors that are easy to count and happen at a relatively low frequency. For example, Ginny, the student in the example from Chapter 1, has a targeted skill to "Chart lunch count." For this behavior, the observer could collect data on a target behavior of "ask peers what lunch choice (they) want" by placing a tally mark in the box each time the behavior occurs and have a specific number at the end for day-to-day comparison (see Figure 6.3).

---

### *Figure 6.3.* Basic event data recording sheet.

**Event Recording Form**

School:  Anywhere Elementary

Student:  Ginny

Target Behavior: Ask peers what lunch choice (they) want

| Day | Activity | Perform Target Behavior | Total |
|-----|----------|-------------------------|-------|
| Monday | Lunch Count | 7HH 7HH 7HH 7HH 7HH | 25 |
| Tuesday | "            " | 7HH 7HH 7HH 7HH //// | 24 |
| Wednesday | "            " | 7HH 7HH 7HH 7HH 7HH | 25 |
| Thursday | "            " | 7HH 7HH 7HH 7HH /// | 23 |
| Friday | "            " | 7HH 7HH 7HH 7HH 7HH | 25 |
| Total for Week | _____ | _____ | 122 |

---

Alternatively, when using event recording, the teacher may decide that a comparison or collecting information on the percentage of occasions when the behavior occurs is necessary. In this case, the data collection sheet would be slightly different, in that it would include a space for listing opportunities to perform a given behavior as well as a space for recording actual performance, leading to a percentage rather than a number for comparison purposes (see Figure 6.4).

Again, in the case of Ginny, one of her targeted behaviors is to use her interactive language board. Just having information on use would not tell the whole story. More information is gained from collecting data on both the opportunities to use the board and her actual usage. This percentage leads to a more appropriate picture of her behavior.

**Figure 6.4. Event recording sheet with comparison.**

### Event Recording Form

School: Anywhere Elementary          Date: 2-23-07

Student: Ginny

Target Behavior: Use interactive language board

| Time | Activity | Opportunity to Perform Behavior | Performed Behavior | Percentage Achieved |
|------|----------|--------------------------------|--------------------|---------------------|
| 7:30-7:55 | Breakfast | 𝓣𝓗𝓛 𝓣𝓗𝓛 𝓣𝓗𝓛 | 𝓣𝓗𝓛 //// | 9/15= 60% |
| 8:05-8:20 | Independent morning work | 𝓣𝓗𝓛 𝓣𝓗𝓛 | 𝓣𝓗𝓛 /// | 8/10=80% |
|  |  |  |  |  |
|  |  |  |  |  |
|  |  |  |  |  |

Lastly, another type of event recording data collection sheet may be used if the concern is the level of prompting necessary for the target behavior to occur. This type of data can be used to assist in planning for gradually decreasing the level of prompting needed. An example of this for Ginny is monitoring of transitions (see Figure 6.5).

## *Figure 6.5.* Prompt level event recording sheet.

School: Anywhere Elementary        Date: 8-23-07

Student: Ginny

Target Behavior: Use transition data sheet

Schedule Present: <u>Y</u>     N        Schedule in Use:     <u>Y</u>     N
Schedule Type:     Stationary     <u>Mobile</u>
Schedule Steps:    1. "Check Schedule"  <u>Put picture in finished pocket</u>
                   2. <u>Pull next picture off</u>
                   3. <u>Put in the work area</u>
                   4. <u>Go to designated area</u>
                          5. <u>Complete activity</u>

| Activity 1: _____ | *Step* | *Status/Prompting* | | | | |
|---|---|---|---|---|---|---|
| | 1 | I | V | G | M | P |
| | 2 | I | V | G | M | P |
| | 3 | I | V | G | M | P |
| | 4 | I | V | G | M | P |
| | 5 | I | V | G | M | P |
| | | | | | | |
| Activity 2: _____ | *Step* | *Status/Prompting* | | | | |
| | 1 | I | V | G | M | P |
| | 2 | I | V | G | M | P |
| | 3 | I | V | G | M | P |
| | 4 | I | V | G | M | P |
| | 5 | I | V | G | M | P |
| | | | | | | |
| Activity 3: _____ | *Step* | *Status/Prompting* | | | | |
| | 1 | I | V | G | M | P |
| | 2 | I | V | G | M | P |
| | 3 | I | V | G | M | P |
| | 4 | I | V | G | M | P |
| | 5 | I | V | G | M | P |

*Note.* I=Independent; V=Verbal; G=Gesture; M=Model; P=Put through.

*Latency recording* is another observational system that is also an exact measure of the target behavior. It is used when the goal is to determine how long it takes for the target behavior to occur after the prompt. As an example, if the purpose were to determine how quickly Ginny responded to others/questions by using her language board, one would use a latency recording sheet rather than an event recording sheet. An example of such a sheet may be found in Figure 6.6.

---

### *Figure 6.6.* Latency recording form.

**Latency Recording Form**

School: Anywhere Elementary        Date: 8-23-07

Student: Ginny

Target Behavior: Use interactive language board

| Time | Activity | Time of Prompt | Time Target Behavior Occurred | Latency |
|------|----------|----------------|-------------------------------|---------|
| 7:30-7:55 | Breakfast | 7:31<br>7:35<br>7:45 | 7:33<br>7:36<br>7:47 | 2 minutes<br>1 minute<br>2 minutes |
| 8:05-8:20 | Independent morning work | 8:06<br>8:10 | 8:07:30<br>8:11 | 1-1/2 minutes<br>1 minute |

---

*Duration recording*, a third observational data collection system, is used to keep track of how long a behavior persists. For example, one of Ginny's target behaviors is to "stay next to assigned peer." Figure 6.7 offers a look at what such a sheet might entail.

## Figure 6.7. Duration recording form.

**Duration Recording Form**

School: Anywhere Elementary                     Date: 8-23-07

Student:  Ginny

Target Behavior: Stay next to assigned peer

| Time | Activity | Behavior Began | Behavior Ended | Duration | Total Duration of Behavior for Activity |
|------|----------|----------------|----------------|----------|------------------------------------------|
| 7:30-7:55 | Breakfast | 7:31 7:43 | 7:33 7:48 | 2 minutes 5 minutes | 7 minutes |
| 8:05-8:20 | Independent morning work | 8:06 8:15 | 8:10 8:17 | 4 minutes 2 minutes | 6 minutes |

Duration for Day: _____

**Time sampling**, the last observational data collection system to be addressed here, provides an estimate of the occurrence of the target behavior in instances when the behavior is either ongoing or high-frequency and, therefore, cannot be reliably counted. In time sampling, the person collecting the data records whether the target behavior is or is not occurring at the end of a specific period of time (for example, every 30 seconds) for a specific session (for example, a session of 5 minutes at the beginning of class). While not an exact measure, time sampling is useful for giving an overall picture of a behavior.

In Ginny's case, she has been having difficulty completing work that must be done independently. The teacher decides to collect data on the target behavior of "work independently" for every 15 minutes across activities, checking at the end of every 3 minutes of independent work time to see if Ginny is on task. While this will not give an exact accounting of how much time Ginny is actually working independently, it will give a general estimate of the behavior. Figure 6.8 provides an example of a time sampling data collection sheet.

***Determining when and where data will be collected.*** Once the behavior has been defined and the method for data collection selected, a decision must be made about when and where to collect the data. This decision takes into account the potential influence on the behavior of different environments, different classes/subjects, different groups, different activities, and different teachers. In addition, to maximize the picture of the behavior and the quality of the data obtained, collecting data at different points in time during the day and week may be necessary.

In the CAPS system, data are routinely collected across time, activities, interventions, and environments, thus ensuring ongoing information on student progress, as well as encouraging generalization of the skills as a matter of everyday practice. This prevents failure

## Figure 6.8. Time sampling recording form.

### Time Sampling Recording Form

School: Anywhere Elementary        Date: 8-23-07

Student: Ginny

Target Behavior: Work independently

Session: 15 minutes of each independent work period across activities during the day

Interval: End of every 3 minutes

Activity: Independent morning work, 8:05-8:20

| 3 mins. | 6 mins. | 9 mins. | 12 mins. | 15 mins. |
|---------|---------|---------|----------|----------|
| O | X | X | O | X |

Percent on task at observation point: 40%

Activity: Morning Activities, 8:25-8:50

| 3 mins. | 6 mins. | 9 mins. | 12 mins. | 15 mins. |
|---------|---------|---------|----------|----------|
| X | X | X | O | X |

Percent on task at observation point: 80%

Activity: Special: Computer, 9:10-9:25

| 3 mins. | 6 mins. | 9 mins. | 12 mins. | 15 mins. |
|---------|---------|---------|----------|----------|
| O | X | O | O | O |

Percent on task at observation point: 20%

Activity: Writing, 9:45-10:00

| 3 mins. | 6 mins. | 9 mins. | 12 mins. | 15 mins. |
|---------|---------|---------|----------|----------|
| O | O | X | O | X |

Percent on task at observation point: 40%

X= target behavior occurring     O= target behavior not occurring to track a student's behavior because of missed opportunities. For example, a student might stay on task during morning activities but not during the afternoon. Evaluating what is different during those times (instructional content, time of day, groupings, instructional delivery) and collecting data during different activities assists in pinpointing why a given intervention is or is not effective (Babkie & Provost, 2004).

**_Determining who will collect the data._** In a school setting, it is usually the teacher or paraeducator who collects information on the target behaviors of a given student. However, due to the comprehensive nature of CAPS, anyone working with the student could collect data on various target behaviors as appropriate. Potentially, the lunchroom staff could check Ginny's use of a language board to communicate choices or the school secretary could note the latency between asking Ginny a question and her response. It would certainly include the family to ensure that behaviors are also addressed in out-of-school settings.

Generalization across people, activities, settings, and times remains essential to the student actually mastering a behavior. Additionally, for the student to assume control of his or her behavior, self-monitoring may be determined as an appropriate choice for some or all target behaviors. These decisions would be made by the team.

**_Determining a system for sharing data._** Charting or graphing data to have a visual representation is often the most effective approach to analyzing and sharing data. A visual representation makes it clear what is happening with the behavior, such as when it occurs most often, and that information may be used to assist in reviewing the efficacy of interventions. Anecdotal records accompanying the data can lead to additional reflections on the success of interventions.

A general rule of thumb is to collect data and chart them until a pattern emerges. If the data line is flat, there is no change. If the data line increases or decreases, there is change that may be tied to the intervention. Obviously, if it is a behavior you want more of, an increasing line is a positive, whereas a decreasing line suggests deterioration in the behavior and may indicate that the intervention approach is not effective and that another intervention is warranted. Figure 6.9 is a graph representing the duration data collection of Ginny's target behavior of "stay next to assigned peer" for one day across different activity periods.

***Using information collected for decision making.*** Based on an analysis after data have been collected for a long enough time to determine a pattern, the next step is to develop a plan for future action. For example, the team sees that data collected on Ginny's lunch count indicate that she is consistently doing well on this behavior. Based on those findings, the school team can decide to collect data on another target behavior and just periodically check to see if Ginny's lunch count behavior remains strong. If Ginny was not consistently being successful taking lunch count as shown by her data, a new intervention might be put in place to help her achieve the objective.

### *Figure 6.9.* Graph of Ginny's target behavior: "Stay next to assigned peer."

**Example #1:** Looking at target behavior by days to see if this is the issue.

Number of minutes stayed next to assigned peer out of 45 minutes total (duration recording)

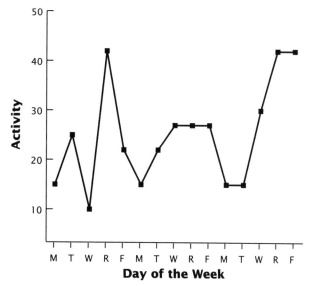

From the trend on this graph, it appears that Ginny has stabilized at 25-30 minutes on W, R, F. M & T appear problematic and need to be investigated as to possible causes.

**Example #2:** Looking at target behavior by activity using percent of time as each activity has different length.

% of time stayed next to assigned peer during activity

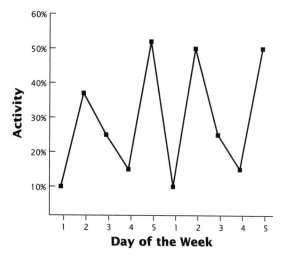

From this graph, it appears that Activities 1 and 4 are the most difficult for Ginny to follow the target behavior, while Activities 2 and 5 are much stronger.

CAPS

# Summary

Collecting data on student behaviors, while sometimes time consuming, is a necessary and efficient way for educators to effect change in their classrooms and increase student achievement. As part of the CAPS systematic approach to intervention, data collection allows the student and the team to measure student success in a routine and systematic fashion.

# References

Babkie, A., & Provost, M. C. (2004). Teachers as researchers. *Intervention in School & Clinic, 39*, 260-268.

Sprick, R. S., & Howard, L. M. (1995). *The teachers' encyclopedia of behavior management: 100 problems/500 plans*. Longmont, CO: Sopris West.

# Generalization

## CHAPTER 7

**A** significant characteristic of students with autism spectrum disorders (ASD) is difficulty generalizing skills and behaviors learned. For example, they learn a skill in one environment and only use the skill in that setting. Or they use a particular strategy only in the presence of the adult who taught them. These issues are illustrated in the following scenario.

*Mr. Meira created a visual support to help Jonathan, a 10-year-old boy with classic autism, learn to use a urinal independently. After several days of instruction, Jonathan used the visual aid without help. Unfortunately, he only used it in the bathroom in Mr. Meira's classroom and did not understand that the toileting routine applied to all bathrooms. Jonathan required additional instruction to use the toileting sequence throughout school and in the community. In addition, each of Jonathan's teachers, including those who taught music and art, had received instruction in how to help Jonathan use his visual support.*

True to its comprehensive nature, the CAPS also addresses this significant issue. Thus, the Generalization column on the CAPS serves to remind adults that supports used in one setting are applicable to others. For example, Tomi's Circle of Friends group (Gold, 1994; Kalyva &

Avramidis, 2005) that occurs during lunch can also happen at recess. The PECS (Frost & Bondy, 2002) that Ling uses in his general education reading class can also be used at recess and in music class.

It is important to consider generalization in planning a student's program. Systematic programming is essential to ensure that a child or youth generalizes newly acquired skills across settings, people, and events. Without this step, the child does not truly possess the skill. Table 7.1 (see also the Appendix) shows examples of how supports may be generalized. Table 7.2 depicts another type of generalization – generalization of skills.

## Table 7.1
### *Generalized Use of Supports*

| CAPS Categories | Support | Is Used During ... | May Also Be Used ... |
|---|---|---|---|
| Structure/ Modifications | ▪ Circling problems to be completed on a work-sheet <br> ▪ Book on tape | ▪ Math <br><br><br><br> ▪ Reading | ▪ Science, reading, social studies, PE, music <br><br> ▪ Social studies, American literature |
| Sensory | ▪ Slant board <br> ▪ Therapy ball | ▪ Language arts <br> ▪ PE | ▪ Math class, art <br> ▪ Reading, math, social studies |
| Social/ Communication | ▪ Social script <br><br><br> ▪ Language board | ▪ Attendance <br><br><br> ▪ Specials | ▪ Academic times for taking surveys, asking a child to play at recess, initiating interactions with members of a cooperative group <br> ▪ Recess, home, lunch |

*Note.* The owner of this book may download a copy of the Generalized Use of Supports form (either Word or pdf format) from www.asperger.net/CAPS
User name: aapc; password: CAPS

**Table 7.2**
*Generalized Skills*

| Skill | Is Used During ... | Can Also Be Used ... |
|-------|--------------------|-----------------------|
| Asking for help | General education academic time | Recess, lunch |
| Using a calculator | Math | Grocery store, bank, school store |
| Interpreting facial expressions | Social skills group | Recess, lunch |
| Taking turns | Circle time | Game playing, PE, home |

# Summary

Generalizing skills learned in one environment or with one person to other environments and persons poses unique challenges for students with ASD. The Generalization column on the CAPS ensures that generalization is built into every phase of the student's program.

**119**

# References

Frost, L., & Bondy, A. (2002). *The Picture Exchange Communication System training manual.* Newark, DE: Pyramid Educational Products.

Gold, D. (1994). We don't call it a 'circle': The ethos of a support group. *Disability & Society, 9,* 435-452.

Kalyva, E., & Avramidis, E. (2005). Improving communication between children with autism and their peers through the 'circle of friends': A small-scale intervention study. *Journal of Applied Research in Intellectual Disabilities, 18,* 253-261.

# Instruction Often Occurring in Specialized Settings

## CHAPTER 8

*With Sheila M. Smith, M.S. and Sherry Moyer, B.S.*

While many strategies and types of support can be effectively implemented in the general education classroom, others require that initial work or perhaps actual instruction take place in a small group or one-on-one outside the general education setting. Many of these strategies are time consuming to implement, but yield results that can ultimately improve the student's skills and independent functioning in multiple environments. These strategies include (a) Circle of Friends; (b) video instruction; (c) Situation, Options, Consequences, Choices, Strategies, Simulation (SOCCSS); (d) social autopsies; (e) Stop, Observe, Deliberate, Act (SODA); (f) cartooning; (g) attribu-

> While many strategies and types of support can be effectively implemented in a general education classroom, others require that initial work or perhaps actual instruction take place in a small group or one-on-one outside the general education setting.

tion retraining; (h) emotion recognition instruction; and (i) Integrated Play Groups.

Following a brief description of these strategies, the idea of skill development is discussed. It is important that once appropriate strategies have been identified a process be in place to ensure that the materials are (a) developed in a timely manner and (b) taught to everybody who will be using them. In addition, it is important that a plan be established for evaluating their effectiveness.

# Circle of Friends

The Circle of Friends strategy is designed to promote social relationships and friendships among children with and without disabilities (Falvey, Forest, Pearpoint, & Rosenberg, 1997; Gold, 1994; Whitaker, Barratt, Joy, Potter, & Thomas, 1998). This systematic process recognizes the positive power of peer groups on individuals who are often marginalized or misunderstood. While often seen as beneficial to students with ASD and related disabilities, Circle of Friends also benefits neurotypical peers who learn different ways of relating to peers and develop an understanding of individual differences (Kalyva & Avramidis, 2005; Schlieder, 2007; Taylor, 1997).

The following steps typically occur in the development of a Circle of Friends (Taylor, 1997):

1. *Establish prerequisites.* The commitment of the school is secured to provide the staff resources necessary (30 to 40 minutes of teacher time to facilitate a small circle group meeting peer

week). Then, the parents and the students who will be in the Circle of Friends are approached, and informed consent and support from the students and their parents is obtained.

2. *Have a class discussion.* A discussion is usually facilitated by an outsider who is familiar with the approach, such as a school psychologist or a speech-language pathologist, with the classroom teacher present. The focus student may or may not be present. Nevertheless, his or her strengths and difficulties are described, and the class members are invited to share their experiences with the focus student and draw some parallels between their own behaviors and those of the focus student. Students are also asked to discuss their experiences with making and keeping friends and how those are similar to or different from the friendship experiences of the focus student. On some occasions, the focus student may be included in this discussion. This decision should be made by the focus student's parents, classroom teacher, and the focus student him/herself, if appropriate. Finally, classmates are asked to make suggestions to assist the child in developing social relationships.

3. *Help class members understand ASD.* Several multimedia materials can help classmates understand ASD. Those include *That's What's Different About Me! Helping Children Understand Autism Spectrum Disorders* (McCracken, 2006) and *Intricate Minds: Understanding Classmates with Asperger Syndrome* (Coulter Video, 2006).

4. *Establish a circle.* A group of six to eight volunteers are selected from students who participated in the class discussion. Myles and

Adreon (2001) recommended that individuals who make up the Circle of Friends be (a) high-status peers (e.g., cheerleader, drill team members, athletes); (b) generally compliant with school rules; (c) socially astute; and (d) genuinely interested in (and, ideally, like) the student with ASD. Moreover, those who participate in the Circle of Friends must value the target student, not merely placate and direct him (Myles & Simpson, 2001). These students become the Circle of Friends for the focus student.

5. *Develop and identify inclusive activities.* The initial meeting of the Circle of Friends group generally takes place immediately after the class discussion and after parent and student consent has been obtained. The facilitator summarizes the class discussion for the focus student, who is subsequently centrally involved in identifying target goals to be worked on and strategies to be implemented. A collaborative approach to problem solving is adopted, and practical arrangements are made. For example, three to four of the volunteers might agree to sit with the focus student at lunch three times per week. Each volunteer might spend a recess period with the student. All might agree to invite her to play games during Friday free-time at school.

> Circle of Friends is an effective approach in enhancing the social interactions of students with ASD and related disabilities.

6. *Hold weekly Circle of Friends meetings.* Weekly meetings are typically held over a period of 6 to 10 weeks. The students and the school staff member responsible (e.g., school psychologist,

speech pathologist) meet weekly to review progress, identify difficulties, and plan practical steps to broaden the social interactions of the focus student. The meetings are carefully managed to be positive and supportive experience for all the students.

Attwood (1998) suggested the use of circles to help children with ASD develop appropriate social behaviors. Circle of Friends has been reported to benefit students with disabilities across age levels (Collins, Ault, Hemmeter, & Doyle, 1996; Haring & Breen, 1992; Hughes et al., 1999; Miller, Cooke, Test, & White, 2003; Taylor, 1997; Whitaker et al., 1998). Thus, Circle of Friends is an effective approach in enhancing the social interactions of students with ASD and related disabilities.

# Video Instruction

Video-based instruction provides individuals with ASD with a structure for acquiring new information that is compatible with their visual learning style. Identified as an evidence-based practice (cf., Ayres & Langone, 2005; Bellini & Akullian, 2007), video instruction can take several forms, including (a) video modeling, creating custom videos using the target child or others as a model; and (b) commercial videos, using professionally created video to teach and/or reinforce skills.

*Video modeling.* The use of a customized video developed using a video camera, a digital camera, or a cell phone is a powerful method of teaching new skills and/or reinforcing previously acquired skills. This strategy allows learning by observing and imitating behaviors in a dynamic format.

Various people such as peers, siblings, parents, teachers, or students themselves may be videotaped as role models (Bellini & Akullian, 2007). The latter, known as video self-modeling, can be particularly successful for an individual with ASD who can watch herself appropriately and successfully performing the target behaviors. Another benefit of video instruction is that the instructor or the learner can pause and replay the videotaped scene repeatedly. This can be helpful to the learner with ASD who requires repeated viewing in order to learn new information.

In addition to teaching new skills, video modeling may be used to reduce anxiety. For example, a child who experiences anxiety related to visiting the school library may benefit from video modeling. The child's teacher can create a brief video showing what students do during library time and use it to prime the child. Video used as a priming strategy (Bellini & Akullian, 2007) can reduce the student's anxiety by creating predictability in the library visit.

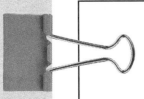

> In addition to teaching new skills, video modeling may be used to reduce anxiety.

***Commercial videos.*** Research has shown that individuals with ASD and related disabilities can learn equally well from videos that depict themselves or others. Many commercial videos have been developed that can be effective in teaching and/or reinforcing skills. Three are outlined below.

- *Joining In! A Program for Teaching Social Skills* (Murdock & Khalsa, 2003) is a multi-video set in which typical peers model target behavior for elementary-age children. A series of lessons targets conversation skills, school skills, and interpersonal skills. The set includes a lesson plan book, follow-up activities, and visual aids.

- *Manners for the Real World: Basic Social Skills* (Coulter Video, 2005) demonstrates how to act during some of the most common interactions between people. Designed for ages from upper-elementary school through adult, the video features clear descriptions and demonstrations of appropriate behavior in the areas of personal hygiene, conversations, introductions, telephone and Internet use, table manners, behavior for ladies and gentlemen, manners in public, serving as a host, and being a guest.

- *The Able Individual Video Learning Series* (Child First, 2005) presents a variety of skills used on a daily basis. Each skill is shown numerous times with decreasing verbal and visual assistance from the individual's point of view. A variety of techniques are used to increase opportunities for success. Areas targeted included hygiene, dressing, and completing chores.

# Situation, Options, Consequences, Choices, Strategies, Simulation (SOCCSS)

Roosa (1995) developed the SOCCSS strategy to help students with social disabilities, including those with ASD, understand social situations and develop problem-solving skills by putting behavioral and social issues into a sequential format. This adult-directed strategy helps children and youth understand cause and effect and realize that they can influence the outcome of many situations by the decisions they make. The strategy may be used one-on-one with a child or can occur as a group activity, depending on the situation and students' needs.

SOCCSS consists of the following six steps.

- *Situation:* After a social problem occurs, the adult helps the child or youth to identify who, what, when, where, and why. The goal is to encourage the child to relate these variables independently. However, at first the adult assumes an active role in prompting and identifying, when necessary, answers to the questions.

- *Options:* The adult and student brainstorm several behavioral options the student might have chosen in the given situation. Brainstorming means accepting and recording all responses without evaluating them. Initially, the adult usually has to encourage the youth to identify more than one option for something that could have been done or said differently.

- *Consequences:* For each behavior option generated, a consequence is listed. The adult asks the student, "So what would happen if you ... *(name the option)*?" Some options may have more than one consequence. It is often difficult for students with ASD to generate consequences because of their difficulty determining cause-and-effect relationships. Role-play at this stage can serve as a prompt in identifying consequences.

- *Choices:* Options and consequences are prioritized using a numerical sequence or a yes/no response. Following prioritization, the student is prompted to select the option that (a) appears doable and (b) will most likely help the student obtain personal wants or needs.

- *Strategies:* A plan is developed to carry out the option if the situation occurs. Although the adult and student collaborate on the stages of the plan, the student should ultimately generate the plan to ensure a feeling of ownership and commitment to use the strategy.

- *Simulation:* Roosa has defined this practice in a variety of ways: (a) using imagery, (b) talking with another about the plan, (c) writing down the plan, or (d) role-playing. The student evaluates personal impressions of the simulation. Did the simulation activity provide the skills and confidence to carry out the plan? If the answer is "no," additional simulation must take place.

Although designed to be used following the occurrence of a social problem, this strategy can also be used as an instructional strategy. For example, teachers can identify problems students are likely to encounter and address them using SOCCSS so that students have a plan prior to a situation occurring (Myles & Simpson, 2001). Figure 8.1 provides a model of the steps of SOCCSS.

***Figure 8.1.* Situation-Options-Consequences-Choices-Strategies-Simulation (SOCCSS) worksheet.**

**SOCCSS Worksheet**

| **Situation** | |
|---|---|
| Who | When |
| What | Why |

| **Options** | **Consequences** | **Choices** |
|---|---|---|
| | | |
| | | |
| | | |
| | | |

| **Strategy – Plan of Action** |
|---|
| |

| **Simulation** | **Select One** |
|---|---|
| 1. Find a quiet place, sit back and imagine how your Situation would work (or not work) based on the various Options and Consequences. | |
| 2. Talk with a peer, staff, or other person about your plan of action. | |
| 3. Write down on paper what may happen in your Situation based on your Options and Consequences. | |
| 4. Practice your Options with one or more people using behavior rehearsal. Start simple and easy for learning. Only make it difficult to test the learning. | |
| 5. ______________________ ______________________ | |

| **Simulation Outcomes** |
|---|
| |

| **Followup** |
|---|
| |

From *Asperger Syndrome and Adolescence – Practical Solutions for School Success* (pp. 112-113), by B. S. Myles and D. Adreon, 2001, Shawnee Mission, KS: Autism Asperger Publishing Company. Reprinted with permission.

# Social Autopsies

This innovative strategy was developed by Lavoie (1994) to help students with social problems understand social mistakes. Simply stated, the social autopsy is a vehicle for analyzing a social skills problem. Specifically, following a social error, the student who committed the error works with an adult to (a) identify the error, (b) determine who was harmed by the error, (c) decide how to correct the error, and (d) develop a plan for preventing the error from occurring again.

A social skills autopsy is not a punishment. Rather, it is a supportive and constructive problem-solving strategy. According to Lavoie (cited in Bieber, 1994), "The autopsy process is particularly effective in enabling the child to see the cause/effect relationship between his social behavior and the reactions of others in his environment" (p. 11). Lavoie posits that the success of the strategy lies in its structure of practice, immediate feedback, and positive reinforcement.

Every adult with whom the student with ASD has regular contact, such as parents, teachers, and therapists, should know how to do a social skills autopsy as a way of fostering student skill acquisition and generalization. Originally designed to be verbally based, the strategy has been modified to include a visual format to enhance student learning. Figure 8.2 provides a worksheet that can be used to structure social autopsies.

***Figure 8.2.*** **Social Autopsies worksheet.**

**Social Autopsies Worksheet**

What happened? ______________________________

______________________________________________

______________________________________________

______________________________________________

| What was the social error? | Who was hurt by the social error? |
|---|---|
| | |
| | |
| | |
| | |

What should be done to correct the error? ______________

______________________________________________

______________________________________________

What could be done next time? ______________________

______________________________________________

______________________________________________

______________________________________________

______________________________________________

______________________________________________

______________________________________________

______________________________________________

______________________________________________

______________________________________________

From *Asperger Syndrome and Adolescence – Practical Solutions for School Success* (p. 109), by B. S. Myles and D. Adreon, 2001, Shawnee Mission, KS: Autism Asperger Publishing Company. Reprinted with permission.

# Stop, Observe, Deliberate, Act (SODA)

Created by Bock (2001) to serve as a social behavioral learning strategy, SODA helps children and youth with ASD and related disabilities "attend to relevant social cues, process these cues, ponder their relevance and meaning, and select an appropriate response during novel social interactions" (p. 273). Similar to social autopsies and SOCCSS, SODA is a visual strategy that has broad application (see Figure 8.3). The strategy, which utilizes the Think Aloud, Think Along model (Andrews & Mason, 1991), contains the following steps.

- *Stop:* This step prompts the individual to develop an organizational schema in which an interaction is to occur. Specifically, the child attempts to define the activities and their order as well as identify a location near the activities from which he can observe to obtain additional information that will help him participate in the activity successfully.

- *Observe:* The point here is to observe the environment for clues to effective and successful intervention. Aspects of the environment targeted for observation may include length of conversations, number of individuals involved in conversations, tone of conversations (i.e., formal, casual), strategies utilized to begin and end conversations, nonverbal language, and any routines that may be in place.

- *Deliberate:* In this phase, the individual with ASD develops a plan for interacting in the new environment. This includes deciding on a topic of conversation, identifying strategies that may lead to successful interactions (i.e., appropriately beginning a conversation, using eye contact, maintaining appropriate social distance), and analyzing how the child thinks she will be perceived by others if she does or does not follow the routines he has identified.

- *Act:* At this point, the child becomes an active participant in the novel environment, carrying out the strategies she identified in the deliberation phase. This stage serves as a platform for generalizing skills that were learned in another environment.

Shown to be effective with children and adolescents with AS (Bock, 2001; Bock, in press a, in press b), SODA is not self-contained but relies on using social skills developed through direct instruction or coaching formats in group or individual settings. SODA's importance lies in the fact that it allows students to approach unique situations without impulse and use social skills in a context that is appropriate.

**Figure 8.3.** Overview of the Stop-Observe-Deliberate-Act (SODA) strategy.

| Acronym Letter | Question to Ask Self |
|---|---|
| **S**top | Where should I go to observe? |
| | What is the room arrangement? |
| | What is the routine or schedule? |
| **O**bserve | What is/are _____ doing? |
| | What is/are _____ saying? |
| | What happens when _____ say and do these things? |
| **D**eliberate | What would I like to do? |
| | What would I like to say? |
| | How will _____ feel when I do and say these things? |
| | How will _____ act when I do and say these things? |
| | Why will _____ act this way? |
| **A**ct | When I go to _____ I plan to:<br>(a)<br>(b)<br>(c)<br>(d) |

# Cartooning

Visual symbols such as cartooning have been found to enhance the ability of persons across the autism spectrum to understand their environment (Hagiwara & Myles, 1999; Kuttler, Myles, & Carlson, 1998; Rogers & Myles, 2001). Used as a generic term, cartooning has been implemented by speech-language pathologists for many years to enhance social understanding and problem solving in their clients. Cartoon figures play an integral role in several intervention techniques, including pragmaticism (Arwood & Brown, 1999; Arwood & Kaulitz, 2007); mind-reading (Howlin, Baron-Cohen, & Hadwin, 1999); and Comic Strip Conversations™ (Gray, 1995).

According to Attwood (1998), cartooning techniques, such as Comic Strip Conversations™

> allow the child to analyze and understand the range of messages and meanings that are a natural part of conversation and play. Many children with Asperger's syndrome are confused and upset by teasing or sarcasm. The speech and thought bubble as well as choice of colors can illustrate the hidden messages. (p. 72)

Figure 8.4 provides a visual explanation of the sounds that upset Harry, an 8-year-old boy with ASD.

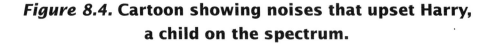

**Figure 8.4.** Cartoon showing noises that upset Harry, a child on the spectrum.

From *Learning with a Visual Brain in an Auditory World. Visual Language Strategies for Individuals with Autism Spectrum Disorders* (p. 42) by E. L. Arwood & C. Kaulitz, 2007. Shawnee Mission, KS: Autism Asperger Publishing Company. Reprinted with permission.

# Attribution Retraining

*by Sherry Moyer, B.S.*

A key element to positive social interactions is the ability to accurately assess the situation. To do so, we ask ourselves questions like "What is happening right now?" "Why should I do this?" or "What does he/she need from me?" Usually the answers are concrete or so obvious that they pose no major challenge.

However, other questions may be much more difficult to answer. Such questions include "Why is this happening to me?" "Why did she say that?" "Why are they behaving that way?" To judge our own well-being and select an appropriate response, we must look for insight about or understanding of other people's motivations, thoughts, words, and deeds. Individuals with ASD have challenges in this area, and when coupled with documented difficulties in regulating sensory input while responding to emotional situations, it is easy to see how quickly a simple social interaction can go wrong.

Attribution retraining is a cognitively oriented process that allows for an unemotional assessment of the circumstances using three very specific parameters developed by Weiner (1986). Weiner's research focused on how students with special needs attributed the circumstances of their successes and failures. He found that students use the following three parameters to determine their circumstances:

1. **Is this situation internal or external to me?** In other words, is it directly related to something about me as a person, such as my height or dislike of certain foods or special interests?

2. **Is the situation stable or unstable?** Do I find myself in the same circumstances every time I do this?

3. **Is the situation controllable or uncontrollable?** Is there any way that I can have a positive influence or effect on the outcome of my circumstances? Can I get my needs met without hurting others? (see Figure 8.5).

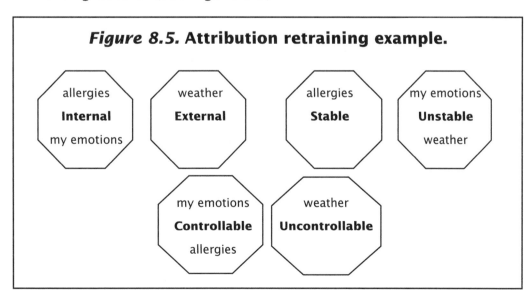

**Figure 8.5. Attribution retraining example.**

In general, Weiner found that most students in his study attributed their circumstances as being internal to them, stable, and uncontrollable. Such a pattern of assessing a situation leaves a person with very little incentive to expend any effort and with no particular motivation to try to make things better. For instance, if you thought that every time you took a math test you would fail because you are not smart enough, or because you thought the teacher did not like you, you would very likely not be motivated or optimistic that you could positively influence your outcomes. One study of adolescents with Asperger Syndrome revealed these very same patterns of depressed attributions (Barnhill & Myles, 2001). Hence the importance of attribution retraining.

Attribution retraining includes the following three steps:

Step 1: To help students retrain their attribution patterns, use the diagram in Figure 8.5 to practice assigning ideas or concepts to each of the three parameters. Be sure to start with concrete ideas such as age, gender, noise in a room, schedules, etc., to give students an opportunity to learn the actual process of attribution. Remember to use terms that the students are familiar with or ideas that are relevant to their life.

Step 2: Once it is clear that the student has learned the process by using concrete ideas or terms, gradually introduce more abstract concepts. After you have determined that the student is able to label abstract ideas or concepts, offer sample social situations that can be analyzed. Work together to define the situation and then cover the three parameters.

Step 3: Over time, encourage students to take more leadership in analyzing the situation and identifying their assessment of the circumstances as being positive or negative. The rule is that the more positive the assessment is, the more motivated students will be to take action. If all goes well, over time students should be able to use this strategy effectively enough so that they can improve their interactions by consistently selecting appropriate responses.

# Emotion Recognition Instruction (*Mind Reading*)

While emotion recognition (ER) challenges in individuals with ASD have been widely recognized (APA, 2000; Barnhill, 2001), few materials have been developed to address this issue. The primary instructional support used to develop emotion and mental state recognition is *Mind Reading* (Baron-Cohen, Golan, Wheelwright, & Hill, 2004), a multimedia computer software program. The program provides a structured and systematic approach to learning emotion recognition in face and voice.

*Mind Reading* is made up of three main components: the Emotions Library, the Learning Center, and the Games Zone. The software also includes quizzes to test progress. A home screen organizes the components and is the starting point for the program. There is also a log-in screen to use once users have chosen which area they wish to start with during a given session. Throughout the program, on the bottom of the screen is a navigation bar that allows the user to quickly see and move to various parts of the program.

Adults have the ability to control settings of the software, including volume level, availability of rewards, difficulty level, word screening, quiz characteristics, and so forth. Quizzes may also be controlled in terms of the type of questions asked, the number of correct responses required before rewards were earned, and the level of words used.

This multimedia technology has been used successfully to teach basic and complex ER to adults and children (Golan, 2006; Golan & Baron-Cohen, 2006a, 2006b; LaCava, Golan, Baron-Cohen, & Myles, in press).

# Integrated Play Groups

Another way to foster positive peer relationships is to create integrated play groups. Pamela Wolfberg's guide *Peer Play and the Autism Spectrum* (2003) is an excellent resource for developing and implementing integrated play groups. Briefly, play groups involve "expert" and "novice" players engaging in play with the support of a "play guide." As "novice" players, individuals with ASD need opportunities to learn from "expert" peer players. Play groups occur in a natural setting and are facilitated by a trained play guide. Play groups work best when a play guide creates an action plan and prepares various supports ahead of time.

# Table 8.1
## *Integrated Play Groups*

### Steps for Integrated Play Groups

1. Provide visual supports that state what the game plan is for the facilitated play session. Visuals can be pictures or written cues but should be used to guide the play and keep a clear focus. Turn-taking visual supports should be provided if a board game is being played or if children are struggling to take turns with blocks, cars, etc. Play guides should prepare visual supports before group gets started.

   Suggested visual schedule – play with toys, outside play, play with toys, snack, art/craft time, play with toys, goodbye activity.

2. Prepare the play setting and organize the play materials ahead of time. Limit the number and types of toys that are present so that children are encouraged to play together.

3. Create a list of Play Group Rules:

   Be nice to your friends; Be nice to the toys; Ask for help; Play together

4. Provide support and facilitate the group.

### A Play Guide's Role During Integrated Play Groups

1. Review the rules and the visual schedule for the play group before play begins.

2. Follow the children's lead but set the tone for how the players treat each other and include everyone.

3. Direct children to the visual supports to aid in transitions and support play.

4. Build in routines and rituals (particularly at the beginning and end of the play group – sometimes a song or chant works great).

5. Be sure to direct the children to each other; they should not keep coming to you and asking you questions.

6. Scaffold the play.

7. Set up arts/crafts as cooperative arrangements whenever possible so that children get used to interacting with each other. For example, have one child in charge of the scissors, one child in charge of the paper, one child in charge of the glue sticks, etc. Then prompt the children to ask, "Who needs glue?" etc.

8. Even when play is going great, be nearby "just in case" to ensure the group stays successful.

# Development of Supports

Many skills that are used in a general education setting require significant preparation time – time that is often not available to classroom teachers. Thus, special educators, related services personnel, and paraprofessionals often must assume the responsibility for developing and/or identifying supports that are needed by children and youth with ASD. They may also have to teach the student, and perhaps the general education teacher, how and when to use the support. Visual schedules, task cards, sensory supports, slant boards, and communication systems (i.e., language boards, Picture Exchange Communication System [Frost & Bondy, 2002]) are samples of supports that are often personally developed and/or selected for specific students.

When completing a CAPS, it is important to designate not only what supports need to be developed and/or selected, but also (a) who will develop them, (b) who will teach use of the support, and (c) how and when its effectiveness will be evaluated. Table 8.2 (see also the Appendix) provides a sample CAPS Support Development Form.

### Table 8.2
#### Sample CAPS Support Development Form

| Support | Who Will Develop Support | Date Support Needed | Who Will Teach Support Use | When to Evaluate Effectiveness | How to Evaluate Effectiveness |
|---------|--------------------------|---------------------|----------------------------|--------------------------------|-------------------------------|
|         |                          |                     |                            |                                |                               |
|         |                          |                     |                            |                                |                               |
|         |                          |                     |                            |                                |                               |
|         |                          |                     |                            |                                |                               |

*Note.* The owner of this book may download a copy of the CAPS Support Development form (either Word or pdf format) from www.asperger.net/CAPS
User name: aapc; password: CAPS

Students with ASD often require extensive instruction in an individualized or small-group setting to learn skills that can benefit them in multiple environments. In many cases, such instruction is a prerequisite for academic, social, and behavior success. For example, for the many students who experience challenges with detecting anxiety in themselves, instruction on using the Incredible 5-Point Scale (Buron & Curtis, 2004) in a one-on-one setting may precede successful social interactions on the playground.

## Summary

Not only is special instruction required for students with ASD, but they often need individualized materials to be successful across multiple environments. Visual schedules, homework checklists, and reminder cards are just a few examples of the materials students may need. Although used in general education and community settings, these supports are most likely developed by special education or related services personnel outside of the environment in which they will eventually be used. Both extensive instruction and specialized supports are needed as a part of the CAPS process. A plan must be designed to ensure that they are in place.

# References

American Psychiatric Association. (2000). *Diagnostic and statistical manual for mental disorders* (4th ed., text revision). Washington, DC: Author.

Andrews J. F., & Mason, J. M. (1991). Strategy usage among deaf and hard of hearing readers. *Exceptional Children, 57,* 536-545.

Arwood, E., & Brown, M. M. (1999). *A guide to cartooning and flowcharting: See the ideas.* Portland, OR: Apricot.

Arwood, E. L., & Kaulitz, C. (2007). *Learning with a visual brain in an auditory world: Visual language strategies for individuals with autism spectrum disorders.* Shawnee Mission, KS: Autism Asperger Publishing Company.

Attwood, T. (1998). *Asperger's syndrome: A guide for parents and professionals.* London: Jessica Kingsley.

Ayres, K. M., & Langone, J. (2005). Intervention and instruction with video for students with autism: A review of the literature. *Education and Training in Developmental Disabilities, 40,* 183-196.

Baron-Cohen, S., Golan, O., Wheelwright, S., & Hill, J. J. (2004). *Mind Reading: The interactive guide to emotions.* London: Jessica Kingsley.

Barnhill, G. P. (2001). Social attribution and depression in adolescents with Asperger syndrome. *Focus on Autism and Other Developmental Disabilities, 16,* 46-53.

Barnhill, G. P., & Myles, B. S. (2001). Attributional style and depression in adolescents with Asperger Syndrome. *Journal of Positive Behavior Interventions, 3,* 175-183.

Bellini, S., & Akullian, J. (2007). A meta-analysis of video modeling and video self-modeling interventions for children and adolescents with autism spectrum disorders. *Exceptional Children, 73,* 264-287.

Bieber, J. (1994). *Learning disabilities and social skills with Richard LaVoie: Last one picked ... first one picked on.* Washington, DC: Public Broadcasting Service.

Bock, M. A. (2001). SODA strategy: Enhancing the social interaction skills of youngsters with Asperger syndrome. *Intervention in School and Clinic, 36,* 272-278.

Bock, M. A. (in press a). A social behavioral learning strategy intervention for a child with Asperger syndrome: A brief report. *Remedial and Special Education,* 28(3).

Bock, M. A. (in press b). The impact of social behavioral learning strategy training on the social interaction skills of four students with Asperger syndrome. *Focus on Autism and Other Developmental Disabilities.*

Buron. K. D., & Curtis, M. (2003). *The incredible 5-point scale.* Shawnee Mission, KS: Autism Asperger Publishing Company.

Child First. (2005). *The able individual video learning series.* Yardley, PA: Author.

Collins, B., Ault, M., Hemmeter, M., & Doyle, P. (1996). Come play! *Teaching Exceptional Children, 29,* 16-21.

Coulter Video. (2005). *Manners for the real world: Basic social skills.* Winston-Salem, NC: Author.

Coulter Video. (2006). *Intricate minds: Understanding classmates with Asperger syndrome.* Winston-Salem, NC: Author.

Bellini, S., & Akullian, J. (2007). A meta-analysis of video modeling and video self-modeling interventions for children and adolescents with autism spectrum disorders. *Exceptional Children, 73,* 264-287.

Falvey, M., Forest, M., Pearpoint, M., & Rosenberg, R. (1997). *All my life's a circle.* Toronto, Canada: Inclusion Press.

Frost, L., & Bondy, A. (2002). *The Picture Exchange Communication Systems training manual.* Newark, DE: Pyramid Educational Products.

Golan, O. (2006). *Systemising emotions: Teaching emotion recognition to people with autism using interactive multimedia.* Unpublished doctoral dissertation, University of Cambridge, Cambridge.

Golan, O., & Baron-Cohen, S. (2006a). Systemizing empathy: Teaching adults with Asperger syndrome or high functioning autism to recognize complex emotions using interactive media. *Development and Psychopathology, 18,* 591-617.

Golan, O., & Baron-Cohen, S. (2006b). *Teaching children with Asperger syndrome and high functioning autism to recognize emotions using interactive multimedia.* Unpublished manuscript.

Gold, D. (1994). We don't call it a 'circle': The ethos of a support group. *Disability & Society, 9,* 435-452.

Gray, C. (1995). *Social stories unlimited: Social stories and comic strip conversations.* Jenison, MI: Jenison Public Schools.

Hagiwara, T., & Myles, B. S. (1999). A multimedia social story intervention: Teaching skills to children with autism. *Focus on Autism and Other Developmental Disabilities, 14,* 82-95.

Haring, T., & Breen, C. (1992). A peer-mediated social network intervention to enhance the social integration of persons with moderate and severe disabilities. *Journal of Applied Behavior Analysis, 25,* 319-333.

Howlin, P., Baron-Cohen, S., & Hadwin, J. (1999). *Teaching children with autism to mind-read: A practical guide.* London: Wiley.

Hughes, C., Guth, C., Hall, S., Presley, J., Dye, M., & Byers, C. (1999). "They are my best friends," Peer Buddies promote inclusion in high school. *Teaching Exceptional Children, 31,* 32-37.

Kalyva, E., & Avramidis, E. (2005). Improving communication between children with autism and their peers through the 'circle of friends': A small-scale intervention study. *Journal of Applied Research in Intellectual Disabilities, 18,* 253-261.

Kuttler, S., Myles, B. S., & Carlson, J. K. (1998). The use of social stories to reduce precursors of tantrum behavior in a student with autism. *Focus on Autism and Other Developmental Disabilities, 13,* 176-182.

LaCava, P. G., Golan, O., Baron-Cohen, S., & Myles, B. S. (in press). Using assistive technology to teach emotion recognition to students with Asperger Syndrome: A pilot study. *Remedial and Special Education.*

McCracken, H. (2006). *That's what's different about me! Helping children understand autism spectrum disorders.* Shawnee Mission, KS: Autism Asperger Publishing Company.

Miller, M. C., Cooke, N. L., Test, D. W., & White, R. (2003). Effects of friendship circles on the social interactions of elementary age students with mild disabilities. *Journal of Behavioral Education, 12,* 167-184.

Murdock, L., & Khalsa, G. S. (2003). *Joining in! A program for teaching social skills.* Shawnee Mission, KS: Autism Asperger Publishing Company.

Myles, B. S., & Adreon, D. (2001). *Asperger Syndrome and adolescence: Practical solutions for school success.* Shawnee Mission, KS: Autism Asperger Publishing Company.

Myles, B. S., & Simpson, R. L. (2001). *Asperger syndrome: A guide for educators and parents* (2nd ed.). Austin, TX: Pro-Ed.

Rogers, M. F., & Myles, B. S. (2001). Using social stories and comic strip conversations to interpret social situations for an adolescent with Asperger syndrome. *Intervention in School and Clinic, 36,* 310-313.

Roosa, J. B. (1995). *Men on the move: Competence and cooperation: Conflict resolution and beyond.* Kansas City, MO: Author.

Schlieder, M. (2007). *With open arms – Creating school communities for kids with social challenges using circle of friends, extracurricular activities, and learning teams.* Shawnee Mission, KS: Autism Asperger Publishing Company.

Taylor, G. (1997). Community building in school: Developing a circle of friends. *Educational and Child Psychology, 14,* 45-50.

Weiner, B. (1986). *An attributional theory of motivation and emotion.* New York: Springer-Verlag.

Whitaker, P., Barratt, P., Joy, H., Potter, M., & Thomas, G. (1998). Children with autism and peer group support: Using "Circle of Friends." *British Journal of Special Education, 25,* 60-64.

Wolfberg, P. (2003). *Peer play and the autism spectrum.* Shawnee Mission, KS: Autism Asperger Publishing Company.

147

# M-CAPS – Using CAPS in Middle School, High School, and Beyond

## CHAPTER 9

**T**he structure of middle/high school is different from the structure of the elementary grades. At the elementary level, students often remain in the same setting or infrequently move from class to class, except for some specials. The schedule in middle school and high school is totally different, however. Here the school day is structured by time and subject, and students often move from room to room each hour with brief stops at their lockers in between.

This chapter overviews how CAPS can still be used in middle and high school but with some modifications. That is, while the traditional CAPS works for some courses, it is not applicable to others. This is where the M-CAPS comes in. While basically the same, the Modified Comprehensive Autism Planning system differs somewhat in structure from the form used during the elementary years.

# The Comprehensive Autism Planning System

Some classes in middle and high school mirror in structure those that are taught in elementary school. For these classes, the traditional CAPS may be used. Physical education is an example of a class that does not follow the aforementioned structure, and for which the CAPS by time and activity would be most appropriate. Students who have work experiences, community-based opportunities, and extracurricular activities would also have a traditional CAPS completed for these classes. Figure 9.1 provides a sample CAPS for a middle school PE class.

# The Modified Comprehensive Autism Planning System (M-CAPS)

When students enter middle and high school, most change rooms and teachers for each class. They may have as many as nine teachers in nine different classrooms during a typical school day. Despite their movement from classroom to classroom, the activities in which students participate in each academic class are similar. That is, in each class students are likely to be required to participate in a mixture of (a) independent work, (b) group work, (c) tests, (d) lectures, and (e) homework. From this standpoint, the activities in English class and geometry are the same.

The M-CAPS is an effective means of communicating to educators who teach academic subjects the types of supports students need during each activity (Sue Klingshirn, personal communication, April, 23, 2006).

## Figure 9.1. Sample CAPS for nonacademic class in middle/high school.

### Sample CAPS for Nonacademic Class in Middle/High School

| Activity | Targeted Skills to Teach | Structure/ Modifications | Data Collection | Reinforcement | Social Skills/ Communication | Sensory Strategies | Generalization |
|---|---|---|---|---|---|---|---|
| **PE** | ▪ Participation in group sports<br>▪ Accepting loss | ▪ Calendar of competitive sports<br>▪ Run errands, as needed (behavior: space invasion, loud voice; when game ends)<br>▪ Review sportsmanship guidelines (with entire class) using cue cards<br>▪ Present miniature cue card at 5-minute warning | ▪ Time in PE<br>▪ Number of meltdowns | ▪ Participation<br>▪ Accepting loss (Use reinforcement menu)<br>▪ Social reinforcer | ▪ Game statistician<br>▪ Peer buddy<br>▪ Social Story™ | ▪ Ear plugs<br>▪ Calming cards<br>▪ Sensory breaks<br>▪ Stress Thermometer | Accepting loss during board games at home |

The multidisciplinary team that plans the program for a high school student with ASD who spends extensive time in general education classrooms develops the student's program using the M-CAPS. As a result, each of the student's academic teachers shares the same document. The M-CAPS used in biology is the same as the M-CAPS used in sociology. The supports are the same. Figure 9.2 provides a blank copy of the M-CAPS form (see also the Appendix); Figure 9.3 provides a sample completed M-CAPS for middle/high school academic classes.

The benefits of using the M-CAPS in middle and high school are many, and include the following.

- The student uses the same types of supports across classes, which allows her to see the flexibility of supports, which in turn facilitates her understanding of the concept of generalization (i.e., "Whenever I am stressed I can use my coping cards. It doesn't have to be only in Mr. Miu's room.").

- Communication is fostered across academic teachers because teachers share the same documents and have access to the same types of supports for a given student.

- The student's case manager and team can easily track successes and problems across academic subjects. For example, if Susan is experiencing problems during independent work in psychology, the team can consult Susan's other academic teachers to identify whether problems also exist with independent work in their classes.

Thus, the M-CAPS is an efficient way to determine and implement supports across academic subjects.

## Figure 9.2. Blank M-CAPS.

## Modified Comprehensive Autism Planning Systems (M-CAPS)
## for Middle and High School Students

| Activity | Targeted Skills to Teach | Structure/ Modifications | Reinforcement | Sensory Strategies | Social Skills/ Communication | Data Collection | Generalization |
|---|---|---|---|---|---|---|---|
| Independent Work | | | | | | | |
| Group Work | | | | | | | |
| Tests | | | | | | | |
| Lectures | | | | | | | |
| Homework | | | | | | | |

*Note.* The owner of this book may download a copy of the M-CAPS form (either Word or pdf format) from www.asperger.net/CAPS User name: aapc; password: CAPS

## Figure 9.3. Sample M-CAPS.

## Modified Comprehensive Autism Planning Systems (M-CAPS) for Middle and High School Students

| Activity | Targeted Skills to Teach | Structure/ Modifications | Reinforcement | Sensory Strategies | Social Skills/ Communication | Data Collection | Generalization |
|---|---|---|---|---|---|---|---|
| **Independent Work** | Task completion | ▪ Task organizer *(prompt to use)* <br>▪ Organization calendar *(prompt to use)* <br>▪ Systematic fading procedures for independent use <br>▪ Peer buddies | Completing homework/in-class work *(from reinforcement menu)* | ▪ Relaxation techniques <br>▪ Coping Cards <br>▪ Ear plugs <br>▪ Stress Thermometer | Asking for help when stuck | ▪ Task organizer <br>▪ Organization calendar | Completing homework |
| **Group Work** | Conversational rules | ▪ Task organizer *(prompt to use)* <br>▪ Organization calendar *(prompt to use)* <br>▪ Systematic fading procedures for independent use <br>▪ Peer buddies | ▪ Completing homework/in-class work *(from reinforcement menu)* | ▪ Relaxation techniques <br>▪ Coping cards <br>▪ Stress Thermometer | ▪ Conversation cues <br>▪ Hidden curriculum notebook <br>▪ Cues for commenting and asking questions <br>▪ Social Story™ about group work | ▪ Task organizer <br>▪ Organization calendar | Lunch conversation |
| **Tests** | Task completion | ▪ Task organizer *(prompt to use)* <br>▪ Organization calendar *(prompt to use)* <br>▪ Systematic fading procedures for independent use | ▪ Calming skills <br>▪ Appropriate conversation <br>▪ Test completion *(from reinforcement menu)* | ▪ Relaxation techniques <br>▪ Coping cards <br>▪ Stress Thermometer | Cues for commenting and asking questions | ▪ Task organizer <br>▪ Organization calendar | ▪ Turning in assignments <br>▪ Working independently |
| **Lectures** | Attention to task | ▪ Task organizer *(prompt to use)* <br>▪ Organization calendar *(prompt to use)* <br>▪ Systematic fading procedures for independent use | ▪ Calming skills <br>▪ Appropriate conversation *(from reinforcement menu)* | ▪ Relaxation techniques <br>▪ Coping cards <br>▪ Stress Thermometer | ▪ Conversation cues <br>▪ Comic Strip™ Conversations <br>▪ Hidden curriculum notebook <br>▪ Cues for commenting and asking question | ▪ Task organizer <br>▪ Organization calendar | Listening during group work |
| **Homework** | ▪ Task completion <br>▪ Materials and supplies needed | ▪ Homework checklist *(prompt to use and double check with student)* | ▪ Homework turned in *(from reinforcement menu)* | ▪ Relaxation techniques <br>▪ Stress Thermometer | NA | Homework turned in complete | Turning in classwork |

# And Beyond ...

The M-CAPS can also be a valuable tool beyond high school. For example, students with ASD who enter a two- or four-year college or university may find that the M-CAPS provides the type of structure they need to be successful in their classes. The M-CAPS easily communicates what the student needs to be successful across activities and may be shared with Office of Disabilities staff and college professors. In addition, it supports student self-advocacy. That is, students with ASD can approach faculty members with the M-CAPS and use it as a starting point to discuss student strengths and needs.

## Summary

The CAPS and M-CAPS are tools that can be used across a student's school years. They are just as applicable in first grade as in 12th grade. Further, they may be used in college settings as structured self-advocacy tools that allow the student to have supports in place to facilitate academic success.

# The CAPS Process

## CHAPTER 10

**A**s illustrated throughout the book, CAPS is designed to examine a student's program and build upon the supports and strategies that are in place. In addition to understanding the CAPS system itself, it is important to know how to develop the CAPS. The purpose of this chapter is to discuss how to facilitate the development of CAPS by an educational team.

For the best results, as many team members as possible should participate, including (a) student, (b) parents, (c) general education teacher, (d) special education teacher, (e) intervention specialist, (f) paraprofessional, (g) speech-language pathologist, (h) speech language pathologist, (i) occupational therapist, (j) school psychologist, (k) guidance counselor, (l) school administrator, (m) regional education support personnel, as well as others.

This chapter provides a structure to facilitate the development of a CAPS. Specifically, it defines the roles of those participating on a CAPS team and outlines what each does to design an effective CAPS.

## Team Member Roles

Team members assume one of three roles: facilitator, recorder, or team member. Team member roles are outlined in Table 10.1.

# Table 10.1
## *Team Member Roles*

**Facilitator**

1. Who is the facilitator?

   This person is usually a current team member with a general understanding of the student. It may be the school psychologist, general educator, special educator, speech-language pathologist, occupational therapist, physical therapist, parent, or anyone with a vested interest in the student's education.

2. What is the role to the facilitator?

   - Explains the process

   - Enlists team members

   - Ensures that all team members take ownership of the process and follow through with commitments

**Recorder**

1. Who is the recorder?

   The recorder could be any one of the team members present. The team should choose someone with strong clerical skills. The recorder will be key to making sure the team has good documentation of the student's CAPS and that it is disseminated in a timely manner to all involved.

2. What is the role of the recorder?

   The recorder uses the CAPS form to record the supports for the target student. It is recommended that the recording occur on a computer linked to a projection system. This allows all team members to view the process as it occurs, and the completed documents can be distributed immediately to all team members.

**Team Members**

1. Who are the team members?

   All other individuals on the multidisciplinary team serve in the role of team members.

2. What is the role of the team members?

   All other team members participate in providing information, as well as adding any additional strategies and supports per each area outlined in the CAPS framework.

# Starting the CAPS

Developing a CAPS is a two-step process. The first step consists of developing a baseline CAPS, and the second step involves developing the CAPS that the student will be using daily.

**Step 1: Baseline CAPS.** The baseline CAPS represents the status quo for the student – the place at which the team can begin to look at what additional supports are needed. It is important that, when created, this document becomes a part of the student archives, since it allows for easy identification of student growth.

**Step 2: Daily CAPS.** As detailed in this chapter, the daily CAPS is developed by the team based on the student's need. This CAPS includes supports in all areas, as needed, for all activities across the student's day. This CAPS becomes the student's program.

Planning for a student is a dynamic and multifaceted process. Thus, a team approach is needed. Planning a CAPS can take up to one day, depending on the complexity of student needs and the number and type of supports to be identified. The following provides an overview of the development process.

| Time | Activity | Targeted Skills to Teach | Structure/ Modifications | Reinforcement | Sensory Strategies | Communication/ Social Skills | Data Collection | Generalization Plan |
|------|----------|--------------------------|--------------------------|---------------|--------------------|-----------------------------|-----------------|---------------------|
| 8:00 | Breakfast | | | | | | | |
| | | | | | | | | |

## Time and Activity

***Time.*** *This section indicates the clock time of each activity that the student engages in throughout the day.*

***Activity.*** *Activities include all tasks and activities throughout the day in which the student requires support. Academic periods (i.e., reading, math) nonacademic times (i.e., recess, lunch).*

## Facilitator:

Lead the team in a "virtual" or actual walk through of the student's day.  Start with the moment the student enters the school. Complete these two columns for the entire day before adding ANY supports and strategies.

*Hint*: You may want to have someone play the role of the student and actually move to each activity to be sure you are reporting all activities and transitions.

## Recorder:

Record clock times and name of each activity.  Be sure to ask for clarification if needed.

## Team:

Consider each activity or expectation per each block of time.  There may be more than one activity in a time block.  For example, under circle time you may have the pledge, announcement, singing, etc.

| Time | Activity | Targeted Skills to Teach | Structure/ Modifications | Reinforcement | Sensory Strategies | Communication/ Social Skills | Data Collection | Generalization Plan |
|------|----------|--------------------------|--------------------------|---------------|--------------------|------------------------------|-----------------|---------------------|
| 8:00 | Breakfast | Choose breakfast | | | | | | |
| 8:15 | Calendar – Months – Counting | | | | | | | |

## Skills to Teach

*This may include IEP goals, state standards, and/or skills that lead to school success.*

## Facilitator:

Go across and complete each column of the CAPS. Ask the team to pull specific objectives from the student's IEP, grade-level state standards, and grade-level core curriculum.

## Recorder:

Take note of all objectives, standards, and goals. It will be helpful to denote the type of goal or standard.

- Individualized Education Program (IEP)
- State Standard (SS)
- Grade-Level Curriculum (GLC)

## Team:

Consider what the objective(s) is for each activity. Remember that you have Social/Communication and Sensory columns to complete that may have some of these objectives.

| Time | Activity | Targeted Skills to Teach | Structure/ Modifications | Reinforcement | Sensory Strategies | Communication/ Social Skills | Data Collection | Generalization Plan |
|------|----------|--------------------------|--------------------------|---------------|---------------------|------------------------------|-----------------|---------------------|
| 8:00 | Breakfast | Choose breakfast using breakfast board | Choice board of breakfast items<br><br>Interactive language board<br><br>Visual schedule | | | | | |

### Structure and Modifications (See Chapter 2)

*Structure/Modifications can encompass a wide variety of supports, including placement in the classroom, visual supports (i.e., choice boards, visual schedules), and instructional strategies (i.e., priming, self-monitoring).*

### Facilitator:

To complete this section the team should consider all methodologies in place and additional visual, auditory, physical adaptations that need to be in place for the student to be successful.

*Hint*: You may want to start with the questions provided by TEACCH. According to Mesibov, Shea, and Schopler (2004), the student should be able to answer or know the answer to these questions:

- What activity is the student completing?
- How much does the student need to complete?
- When is he finished?
- What is next?

These questions are answered for the student in the mode he or she is able to receive.

### Recorder:

Bullet all modifications and structures that are in place.

### Team:

Consider additional strategies and methodologies that will provide greater access to the core curriculum.

| Time | Activity | Targeted Skills to Teach | Structure/ Modifications | Reinforcement | Sensory Strategies | Communication/ Social Skills | Data Collection | Generalization Plan |
|------|----------|--------------------------|--------------------------|---------------|--------------------|------------------------------|-----------------|---------------------|
| 8:00 | Breakfast |                        |                          | Choice of food |                   |                              |                 |                     |

## Reinforcement (See Chapter 3)

*Specific types of reinforcement as well as the student's reinforcement schedule are listed under the reinforcement section.*

### Facilitator:

Lead the team in completing a reinforcer assessment.

### Recorder:

Take note of all reinforcing items identified by the team.

### Team:

Consider what the student likes to do in his free time. What is his area of interest? How often is this reinforcement needed?

| Time | Activity | Targeted Skills to Teach | Structure/ Modifications | Reinforcement | Sensory Strategies | Communication/ Social Skills | Data Collection | Generalization Plan |
|------|----------|--------------------------|--------------------------|---------------|--------------------|------------------------------|-----------------|---------------------|
| 8:00 | Breakfast |                        |                          | Choice of food |                   |                              |                 |                     |

## Sensory (See Chapter 4)

*Sensory supports and strategies identified by an occupational therapist are listed in this area.*

### Facilitator:

Review a completed sensory instrument with the team and lead a discussion on sensory issues.

### Recorder:

Record all sensory supports the student needs for each activity.

### Team:

An occupational therapist, using an instrument designed to identify sensory needs, is instrumental in this step. Team members can assist in ensuring sensory supports integrate well within each activity.

| Time | Activity | Targeted Skills to Teach | Structure/ Modifications | Reinforcement | Sensory Strategies | Communication/ Social Skills | Data Collection | Generalization Plan |
|------|----------|--------------------------|--------------------------|---------------|--------------------|------------------------------|-----------------|---------------------|
| 8:00 | Breakfast | | | | | Have additional social language on board (i.e., greetings, questions)<br><br>Work on table manners | | |

## Communication/Social (See Chapter 5)

*Specific communication goals or activities as well as supports are delineated in this section. The speech-language pathologist should provide direction.*

## Facilitator:

Keep in mind that each student has the need for both receptive and expressive communication during each time period. Social interactions should be as natural as possible and match the structure of the activity.

- How does the student express information or needs?
- Is an AAC device needed?
- How does the student receive information?
- Is that method effective?
- How do we know it is working?
- Does the student have opportunities to engage in social interactions with peers and the teacher in class?

## Recorder:

Be sure each time and activity includes a communication and social activity.

## Team:

Ensure that the student has opportunities to communicate and socialize in each activity. Opportunities should match those experienced by peers.

| Time | Activity | Targeted Skills to Teach | Structure/ Modifications | Reinforcement | Sensory Strategies | Communication/ Social Skills | Data Collection | Generalization Plan |
|---|---|---|---|---|---|---|---|---|
| 8:00 | Breakfast | | | | | | Data sheet for choice<br><br>Data on use of language board | |

## Data Collection (See Chapter 6)

*Data collection includes information on the type of data as well as the behavior to be documented during a specific activity. Typically, this section relates directly to IEP goals and objectives.*

## Facilitator:

Lead the team in discussing what data will be collected during each time block. The following questions should be answered:

- How can we embed the data collection?
- Does the data collection method match the resources available in the classroom?
- Does the data collection method match the Skills to Teach?

## Recorder:

Note each form of data collection.

## Team:

Be creative in identifying data collection methods that fit within a classroom routine. Data are often not collected because the data collection method chosen requires materials and personnel not available in the environment.

| Time | Activity | Targeted Skills to Teach | Structure/ Modifications | Reinforcement | Sensory Strategies | Communication/ Social Skills | Data Collection | Generalization Plan |
|------|----------|--------------------------|--------------------------|---------------|--------------------|------------------------------|-----------------|---------------------|
| 8:00 | Breakfast | | | | | | | Use language board during lunch or dinner at home |

### Generalization (See Chapter 7)

*Because individuals with ASD often have problems generalizing information across settings, this section of the CAPS was developed to ensure that generalization of skills is built into the child's program.*

### Facilitator:

Guide the team in answering the following questions:

- How can any of the skills and supports be used at different times of the day and in different environments?
- How can the student be empowered to initiate the skill and use the supports without prompts?

It is often best to begin with one generalization target per activity and gradually add to them over time.

### Recorder:

Ensure that information generated by the team is placed on the CAPS form.

### Team:

Remember that Generalization is the true measure of skill use. This should be an ongoing process. Continue to build generalization into the student's CAPS.

# Summary

In addition to understanding the CAPS system itself, it is important that team members know how to develop the CAPS. Team members assume one of three roles, facilitator, recorder, or team member, all of which are critical to a comprehensive and effective CAPS for the individual student.

# References

Mesibov, G., Shea, V., & Schopler, E. (2004). *The TEACCH approach to autism spectrum disorders*. New York: Klewer Academic Press.

# Case Studies

## CHAPTER 11

**A**s a culmination of the discussion of the CAPS system throughout this book, this chapter presents four case studies to illustrate CAPS in action, three for school and one for home use. The first CAPS describes a program for Mitchell, a preschool student with autism. In the second case study, we meet Sam, who is in an elementary school setting. The third case study introduces Jason, whose CAPS was developed for the home setting. Specifically, this CAPS established an evening routine for his family and him. Finally, Michael's CAPS addresses his needs in high school.

Each of the CAPS provides some pictorial representatives of the supports incorporated in the student's program. In the interest of space, only some of them are included here. In the actual CAPS plan, pictures of all supports would be included.

# Preschool – Mitchell*

### by Yu-Chi Chou, M.S.

Mitchell is a 6-year-old boy. He is attending preschool where he participates primarily in a special education classroom. He was diagnosed with autism at age 3. There are five students in Mitchell's class, served by one teacher and one educational assistant. In addition to his scheduled special education classes, Mitchell participates in group activities with same-age peers in an inclusive setting. He

*Thanks to Judy Halvorson for developing this CAPS.

also receives services from a speech-language therapist and an occupational therapist within his special education classroom setting.

Cognitively, Mitchell matches pictures to items and identifies basic pictures by name and function. He can also identify familiar items by pointing to objects. In addition, Mitchell can complete academic tasks with verbal and visual prompts. Mitchell is functionally nonverbal; he uses gestures and visual cues to communicate. He vocalizes primarily making vowel sounds. Some vocal patterns are easily recognized as well. For example, he makes an "umm" sound for requesting food. Receptively, he is able to use gestures to respond to simple questions, such as "Where is your blue jacket?," and is able to share toys and objects on verbal request. The Picture Exchange Communication System (PECS) is used to improve Mitchell's communication. For example, when requesting a desired item, he assembles a phrase (I want + item) with a picture icon strip to request a desired item from a communication partner.

Mitchell does not play socially interactive games, such as patty-cake, and does not engage in turn taking during play. In addition, he does not play creatively with toys. From a sensory standpoint, Mitchell does not like his head/hair or the back of his neck touched. Deep-pressure brushing is used to provide sensory stimuli. Textured balls and other fidget toys are usually a part of his calming strategies. Motorically, Mitchell can chew food and use an adapted spoon and fork. He can also pull the zipper on his pants up and down. He needs assistance with motor movements, such as climbing on/off a rocking horse.

Mitchell's CAPS was designed to target several group activities that require social interaction. Specifically, the purpose of his CAPS was to improve his integration with other peers, and build on his communication and social skills.

## Strengths

Mitchell can follow short auditory directions with visual prompts. He is also responsive to simple questions. His favorite type of reinforcement is social praise. Mitchell can use gestures to point to objects and express needs. He excels at following routine activities.

## Needs

Mitchell needs systematic prompting to complete activities, such as visual schedules to transition between activities, visual prompts to initiate tasks, and visual organizers to complete academic work. He needs to increase participation in interactive games and imitative play skills with peers. Moreover, he needs to improve communicative skills by continuing his use of PECS.

## Comprehensive Autism Planning System

Mitchell's team did not complete a baseline CAPS. Instead, the team decided to devote their efforts to developing the CAPS to target his half-day preschool program. Specifically, the CAPS addresses the four activities that he participates in daily: recess, Hawaii cultural instruction, lunch, and group play (see Figure 11.1).

## *Figure 11.1.* Mitchells' Comprehensive Autism Planning System (CAPS).

Child/Student: _____ Mitchell _____

| Time | Activity | Targeted Skills to Teach | Structure/ Modifications | Reinforcement | Sensory Strategies | Communication/ Social Skills | Data Collection | Generalization |
|------|----------|--------------------------|--------------------------|---------------|--------------------|-----------------------------|-----------------|----------------|
| 10:00-10:20 | Recess<br>• Sit on rug with peers<br>• Wait to be dismissed<br>• Line up at door<br>• Walk to recess area<br>• Play with peers | • Use hands appropriately<br>• Imitate peers (e.g., playing tag, playing catch with ball)<br>• Stand in line<br>• Walk nicely<br>• Wait your turn<br>• Follow routine verbal directions<br>• Imitate peer in one activity, gradually increasing the length of time for an activity and/or # of activities | • Trained peers<br>• Systematic prompting for independence<br>• Social Story™<br>• Visual mini-schedule | Choice of preferred activities | Keeping Mitchell engaged so he does not put dirt, rocks, and other items in his mouth | • Greeting<br>• Imitation of peers<br>• Social interactive games<br>• Imitate a sequence of two actions<br>• Imitate a novel act in familiar activity | Observation | • Playing with peers at recess<br>• Participation in regular class with peers |
| 10:20-11:00 | Hawaiiana<br>• Discuss lessons and songs with Kupuna. Tape songs and/or video tape class singing song<br>• Teach Mitchell the hand routines or dance to the song before Hawaiian class | • Use hands appropriately<br>• Imitate peers and adults (one of the current songs is the Hokey Pokey in Hawaiian, so Mitchell needs to learn to imitate that dance)<br>• Comply with verbal directions | • Systematic prompting for independence<br>• Visual supports for the sequence of hand, foot, and body | Verbal praise | Calming toys: textured balls or other fidget toys | • Shared attention<br>• Imitate peers in a series of three or more actions<br>• Sit for group activity | Observation | Inclusion in regular class |

## Mitchells' Comprehensive Autism Planning System (CAPS) (cont.)

| Time | Activity | Targeted Skills to Teach | Structure/ Modifications | Reinforcement | Sensory Strategies | Communication Social Skills | Data Collection | Generalization |
|---|---|---|---|---|---|---|---|---|
| 11:00-11:40 | Lunch | • Bite, chew, then swallow food in mouth before scooping next bite<br>• Take one bite of a finger food at a time<br>• Wait between bites<br>• Calm hands while waiting | • Visual sequence of activity<br>• Systematic prompting for independence<br>• Self-monitoring chart | Verbal praise | OT exercises before eating lunch | Eating with others | • Frequency counts of target behaviors | • Eat lunch in cafeteria at school<br>• Eat at home with family<br>• Eat in restaurants or other public places |
| 12:40-13:20 | Group play<br>• Plan for class peers to come to Mitchell's room; practice songs for Hawaiiana<br>• Learn to play with toys and games that are age appropriate<br>• Teach games to play at recess | • Use hands appropriately<br>• Imitate peers<br>• Comply with verbal directions<br>• Imitate a sequence of three or more actions<br>• Imitate a novel act during a familiar activity | • Systematic prompting for independence<br>• Train peers<br>• Play stations to teach how to play with more than one item during an activity period | • Choice of preferred games<br>• Social reinforcement from peers | Calming toys: textured balls or other fidget toys | • Shared attention<br>• Imitate peers and adults<br>• Play creatively with toys<br>• Play routines<br>• Social interactive games | Observation | • Play with peers at recess<br>• Joint group play in community |

Figures 11.2 to 11.6 provide examples of the visual supports that are used throughout Mitchell's program. These support include his daily schedule (see Figure 11.2), recess activities (see Figure 11.3), visual routine for Hawaiian play activity (see Figure 11.4), sensory activity (see Figure 11.5), and task analysis for eating lunch (see Figure 11.6).

**Figure 11.2. Mitchell's daily schedule.**

**Figure 11.3. Mitchell's recess visual schedule.**

**Figure 11.4.** Mitchell's visual routine for Hawaiiana.

**Figure 11.5.** Mitchell's box with sensory fidget toys.

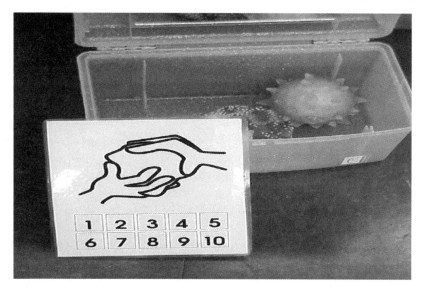

**Figure 11.6.** Mitchell's lunch visual schedule.

# Elementary School – Sam

### By Christina R. Carnahan, Ph.D.

Sam is a 9-year-old male in the second grade. He lives at home with his mother and sister. Sam has autism and a seizure disorder. He currently takes medication for his seizures and hyperactivity. At home, Sam engages in solitary play or large-motor activities with his sister. His mother reports that it is becoming increasingly difficult to take Sam into the community because of safety issues such as running. Her primary concerns include Sam's participation in his community and development of skills that lead to increased independence as he gets older.

Sam attends a large suburban elementary school where he receives all instruction in a special education classroom. His schedule includes one-on-one academic instruction, small-group literacy and language activities, and a variety of gross-motor and sensory breaks embedded in the school day. Sam is functioning at a pre-academic level. Target skills include choice making, increasing verbal skills, and developing self-help skills, such as dressing, following directions, and independently moving through his environment.

Examples of specific academic tasks include matching pictures, sorting by category, and a variety of activities designed to increase his fine-motor skills. Issues related to lack of attention and focus make instruction difficult. It is often unclear if Sam lacks a skills or is simply not focused enough to demonstrate it. For these reasons, Sam often receives instruction in a small room connected to the special education classroom. Finally, Sam's school day includes individual and small-group sessions with the speech-language pathologist, the occupational therapist, and the physical therapist. He does not receive any additional therapies outside of the school day.

In the past year, Sam began vocalizing sounds that approximate words. He is able to verbalize five words, including *bye* and *play*. However, he often needs verbal prompts such as "tell your friends bye" to use these words. He does not yet use these words spontaneously to make requests or interact with others. Sam knows where most items are located in the classroom. He frequently interrupts activities to run to a closet or shelf to obtain the items he wants or needs.

Socialization, independence, and community participation continue to be areas of concern for Sam. At the start of the school year, he engaged in behavior deemed unsafe by the principal. For example, on the playground, Sam wrapped his legs around a little girl while playing on the jungle gym, causing her to fall and hit her head. He also ran from his teachers on several occasions, attempting to engage them in games of chase. Because of these incidences, Sam now has limited access to the rest of the school building and peers. He eats lunch in the classroom, does not go to recess, and has limited access to areas where large groups of children congregate.

These behaviors also influence Sam's participation in the special education classroom. Thus, during small-group activities, an adult always sits behind Sam to prevent him from touching other children. When he transitions from one area of the classroom to another, an adult is always close by, providing a physical prompt by touching Sam on the back or shoulder.

The team feels that Sam has made substantial progress during the last school year but still has significant concerns about behavior, independence, and socialization.

The team completed a baseline CAPS (see Figure 11.7) to determine the interventions already in place. The team had a difficult time articulating target skills for activities, such as arrival, recess, and lunch. For other activities, the target skills were primarily pre-academic and included verbally approximating words related to the calendar and weather, sorting, and matching.

The primary teaching interventions included modeling paired with verbal directions and hand-over-hand prompting. The team also used hand holding as a strategy for managing Sam's behaviors. Despite the hand-holding intervention, Sam continued to wrap his legs around adults and students in the classroom. Sam received one-on-one therapy outside of the classroom from a speech-language pathologist, occupational therapist, and physical therapist for 40 minutes each per week. The team verbally praised Sam when he demonstrated the desired academic skills, such as correctly sorting or matching pictures. They also provided breaks every 5–10 minutes during the one-on-one work sessions.

## Figure 11.7. Baseline CAPS for Sam.

## Baseline: Comprehensive Autism Planning System (CAPS)

Child/Student:  Sam

| Time | Activity | Targeted Skills to Teach | Structure/ Modifications | Reinforcement | Sensory Strategies | Communication Social Skills | Data Collection | Generalization |
|---|---|---|---|---|---|---|---|---|
| 8:50 | Arrival | | Hold S's hand as he walks from the bus to the classroom and while walking around the track | | Walk twice around the track after hanging up backpack | | | |
| 9:15 | Literacy/language group | Put days of the week in order on the calendar | Match pictures of days of the week to pictures on the calendar | Verbal praise | | Verbalize beginning sound for each day of the week | Checklist indicating prompting level for each day of the week | SLP 20 minutes, twice per week |
| 9:30 | Gross-motor/sensory group | Jumping, hopping, standing on one foot | Put cut-out feet on the floor in the classroom | ▪ Drink of water and snack at the end of the activity ▪ Verbal praise | None | | | |
| 10:00 | One-on-one instruction | ▪ Sorting ▪ Matching | Model how to complete the tasks while providing verbal instructions | ▪ Verbal praise ▪ Break every 5–10 minutes | ▪ Weighted vest for 20 minutes ▪ Take breaks in the sensory area | | | |
| 11:30 | Lunch (in classroom with teacher) | | | Verbal praise | None | | | |
| 12:00 | Individual recess | | Hold S's hand as he walks around the track | | Walk five times around the track | | | |
| 12:30 | Greet one peer when he comes to group Literacy/language activity group | Identify the weather when presented with two pictures | Match weather pictures to identical pictures on the weather board | Verbal praise | None | Verbally approximate the words *hi, bye, sunny, windy, cloudy, and raining* | | SLP 20 minutes, twice per week to target sounds for greetings |
| 1:00 | One-on-one Instruction | ▪ Sorting ▪ Matching | Model how to complete the tasks while providing verbal instructions | ▪ Verbal praise ▪ Break every 5–10 minutes | ▪ Weighted vest for 20 minutes ▪ Take breaks in the sensory area | | | |

The team recognized that Sam had a great deal of sensory needs that influenced his participation during the school day. Though the team was unsure about the type of sensory activities that would best meet his needs, they decided to use the track and weighted vest. Sam used the track to take sensory breaks two times during the school day. The paraprofessional took Sam to the track when he arrived at school and during recess. They held hands as they walked slowly around the track, two times in the morning and five times at recess. Sam also wore the weighted vest during the first 20 minutes of each one-on-one instructional session.

## Strengths

Sam has an exuberance for life that he often exhibits in school by darting to and from activities. He wants to have friends and, despite having a limited repertoire of play skills, he continues to initiate interactions with others. Sam's natural curiosity is also evident in the classroom. He is very interested in the materials that are available in the classroom. His language skills are emerging, and he appears to want to use these skills with increasing frequency.

## Needs

The team identified three primary areas of concern for Sam – transitioning, social interactions with others, and increasing attention and focus for learning. The first two areas, transitioning and social interactions, are closely related. Both involve his ability to independently move through the classroom and school environment.

Indeed, Sam's entire school and community experiences are colored by his difficulty transitioning from one area to another. During transitions, Sam may run from the teacher. He may also attempt to wrap his legs or arms around his peers or the teachers. It seems that these rough-and-tumble play behaviors serve as Sam's primary strategy for interacting with others. Not only does such play provide much-needed sensory input, it also allows him to gain the attention of and interact with peers and adults.

Because Sam demonstrates physical behaviors such as those described above, he is rarely in the same learning space as others and has few social interactions or relationships with others. Sam does not appear to understand how his actions (e.g., running away or intruding on others' space) affect others. He also appears to lack the skills to engage others appropriately in games, turn-taking activities, or greetings. During breaks and lunch, he interacts with adults or plays on his own. Staff members watch Sam closely when he is around other children. He needs physical and verbal prompts to maintain his own space or participate in turn-taking activities. For example, during a gross-motor group, each child had the opportunity to swing for 3 minutes. While one child swung, the others sat in their chairs waiting. Sam needed one-on-one adult support to sit in his chair and wait. When asked to transition back to his chair, he needed assistance from two adults to move from the swing to wait.

In addition to the needs described above, Sam's ability to focus and attend to learning materials is a significant area of concern. He is currently able to participate in highly structured one-on-one teaching settings for 2-3 minutes. Even in these situations, he demonstrates sporadic attention to the learning materials. That is, he looks at the materials sometimes but not at other times. It is difficult to determine if Sam lacks a skill in a certain area or if his lack of focus keeps him from demonstrating a specific skill. The team feels that increasing Sam's focus and attention during instructional tasks will significantly improve his skill acquisition.

As mentioned, the primary concerns for Sam include transitioning, social interactions, and attention to academic learning materials. Specific needs include the ability to move from one area to another without adult supports, the ability to interact with others using socially appropriate behaviors, and the ability to focus on (i.e., look at, respond to directions, etc.) a variety of academic learning material. The team identified these three target areas because they believe that improvements in these areas are necessary for and will lead to the development of many other important life skills.

# Comprehensive Autism Planning System

The team collaborated to complete a new CAPS document (see Figure 11.8). They began by identifying important target skills related to each need. These skills were embedded in each activity during the school day. Even activities such as lunch and recess were assigned target skills.

Examples of specific skills include:

- appropriately greeting peers

- waiting for an extended period with decreasing adult support

- turn taking

- self-help skills such as hanging up a jacket or backpack

- appropriate use of playground equipment

- academic-related targets, including communication, working to completion, and attending to learning materials for at least 5 minutes

# *Figure 11.8.* CAPS for Sam.
## Comprehensive Autism Planning System (CAPS)

Child/Student: Sam

| Time | Activity | Targeted Skills to Teach | Structure/ Modifications | Reinforcement | Sensory Strategies | Communication/ Social Skills | Data Collection | Generalization |
|------|----------|--------------------------|--------------------------|---------------|--------------------|-----------------------------|-----------------|----------------|
| 9:00 | Arrival | Entering the school building (walking independently, managing own materials and belongings) | Visual supports, including color-coding, cubby, tape on the floor from school building door to classroom, picture checklist of steps to follow to unpack backpack, video model of a child leaving the bus and walking to the classroom | Tangible (e.g., edibles) reinforcers provided throughout the process; move to the sensory/play area after completing all steps in the process | Weighted backpack (place a few large books in his bag to provide heavy work during this time) | Sam exchanges a greeting with at least two individuals in the hallway; identify the two individuals prior to beginning the process; these individuals approach Sam each morning | Task analysis denoting number and type of prompt(s) for each step in the sequence | • Leaving school independently<br>• Embed OT services to support development of self-care skills |
| 9:15 | Literacy/ language group | • Appropriate greeting<br>• Turn taking<br>• Choosing from a field of three pictures to comment on a book (comment "I see ___" using a voice output device)<br>• Beginning concepts of print | • Visual timer to indicate the amount of time left for the group<br>• Tape on the floor indicating where she should keep his chair, hands, and feet<br>• Visual supports such as a video model to teach appropriate greeting skills (video model shown at start of group to support all group members)<br>• Token board indicating number of turns S must take before he leaves the group | Tangible reinforcers paired with verbal praise for desired behaviors | • Weighted lap pad used as needed<br>• Chewy candy or sucker provided while waiting for his turn to respond | Target skills include appropriate greetings and turn taking | • Checklist: use frequency counts to indicate the number and type of prompts S needs for each skills<br>• Take data on one skill per day (e.g., Monday = greeting, Tuesday = commenting) | |
| 9:30 | Gross-motor/ sensory group | • Turn taking<br>• Attending to and following group directions<br>• Greeting peers<br>• Waiting for at least 2 minutes with decreasing adult prompts | • Visual timer<br>• Tape on the floor to indicate where he should be at all times<br>• Visual directions | • Highly motivating activities such as swinging, bouncing, and jumping<br>• Tangible reinforcers paired with verbal praise for desired behavior such as appropriately transitioning back to his chair | • Weighted lap pad while S waits for his turn.<br>• Fidgets for S to play with while waiting<br>• Heavy work activities for calming before the session begins | • Target social skills: waiting in a chair for his turn and turn taking<br>• Communication: indicate "my turn" verbally or using an augmentative system such as a picture or voice output device | • Chart amount of time S is able to independently wait in a chair<br>• Use frequency counts to indicate type and number of prompts needed for turn-taking activities | Turn taking during games at recess |

## CAPS for Sam (cont.)

| Time | Activity | Targeted Skills to Teach | Structure/ Modifications | Reinforcement | Sensory Strategies | Communication/ Social Skills | Data Collection | Generalization |
|------|----------|--------------------------|--------------------------|---------------|--------------------|------------------------------|-----------------|----------------|
| 10:00 | One-on-one instruction | • Attending to work materials for at least 5 minutes<br>• Following directions<br>• Working to completion<br>• Academic goals and objectives, including specific communication, self-help, and other objectives<br>• Behavioral goals, such as waiting, walking independently from one area to another, following directions | • First/then board indicating "first work, then play"<br>• Tokens to indicate the number of tasks to complete before a break<br>• Placement of desk near the break area | • Choice board that Sam uses to choose what he will work for<br>• High levels of reinforcement: small tangibles (e.g., edibles) provided as he works on a task, with larger reinforcer provided upon completion of a task<br>• Verbal praise for work completion and other desired behaviors | • Frequent sensory/play breaks embedded throughout the work session (e.g., 3 minutes of work, 3-minute break); breaks include structured sensory activities (e.g., deep pressure, heavy work) and free-choice segments<br>• Weighted lap pad used as needed while working<br>• Water bottle with a resistant straw to drink from while working | • Specific language and social skills targets:<br>– indicate preference and answer yes/no questions<br>– Independently initiate a greeting when he comes to the work table<br>– Identify when help is needed and use a picture, sign, or verbal approximation to request help | Create easy-to-use data sheets for each target skills; also collect data on amount of time S attends to work | Use choice board for after-school activities |
| 11:30 | Lunch (in classroom with teacher) | • Following directions<br>• Self-help skills, including eating, opening containers, and washing hands<br>• Communication skills, including requesting help and indicating he is finished using pictures | • Choice board so Sam can request desired items<br>• Color-coded placemats, utensils, bowls, etc., to indicate items that belong to S<br>• Pictures that S can use to indicate when he is finished or needs help | Sam is allowed to choose highly motivating food items; provide these items throughout lunch | • Access to bouncing and swinging before lunch begins<br>• Water bottle with a resistant straw<br>• Weighted utensils<br>• Noise-filtering headphones if S enters the cafeteria | | | |

# CAPS for Sam (cont.)

| Time | Activity | Targeted Skills to Teach | Structure/ Modifications | Reinforcement | Sensory Strategies | Communication/ Social Skills | Data Collection | Generalization |
|------|----------|--------------------------|--------------------------|---------------|--------------------|-----------------------------|-----------------|----------------|
| 12:00 | Individual recess | • Appropriate use of playground equipment, including how to use equipment with others<br>• Staying within a designated space | • Video model to rehearse appropriate use of playground equipment<br>• Stop sign on the gate (be sure the gate is locked before entering the playground) | • Natural reinforcers, such as swinging, jumping, etc.<br>• Tangible reinforcers embedded during transitions | | Target social skills include appropriate use of equipment and interactions with peers while on the equipment | Develop behavioral criteria (e.g., use jungle gym and swings appropriately for five consecutive days before introducing one peer to his recess) | • Gradually include one to two peers in his recess<br>• Gradually group recess by taking walks around the playground when other children are present |
| 12:30 | Literacy/ language activity group | • Appropriate greeting<br>• Turn taking<br>• Choosing from a field of three pictures to comment on a book (e.g., comment "I see ___" using a voice output device)<br>• Beginning concepts of print | • Visual timer to indicate the amount of time left for the group<br>• Tape on the floor indicating where he should keep his chair, hands, and feet<br>• Visual supports, such as a video model to teach appropriate greeting skills (video model shown at start of group to support all group members)<br>• Token board indicating number of turns S must take before he leaves the group. | Tangible reinforcers paired with verbal praise for desired behaviors | • Weighted lap pad used as needed<br>• Chewy candy or sucker provided while waiting for his turn to respond | Target skills include appropriate greetings and turn taking | • Checklist: use frequency counts to indicate the number and type of prompts Sam needs for each skills<br>• Take data on one skill per day (e.g., Monday = greeting. Tuesday = commenting) | |

# CAPS for Sam (cont.)

| Time | Activity | Targeted Skills to Teach | Structure/ Modifications | Reinforcement | Sensory Strategies | Communication/ Social Skills | Data Collection | Generalization |
|------|----------|--------------------------|--------------------------|---------------|--------------------|-----------------------------|-----------------|----------------|
| 1:00 | One-on-one instruction | • Attending to work materials for at least 5 minutes<br>• Following directions<br>• Working to completion<br>• Academic goals and objectives, including specific communication, self-help, and other objectives<br>• Behavioral goals, such as waiting, walking independently from one area to another, following directions | • First/then board indicating "first work, then play"<br>• Tokens to indicate the number of tasks to complete before a break<br>• Placement of desk near the break area | • Choice board that Sam uses to choose what he will work for<br>• High levels of reinforcement: small tangibles (e.g., edibles) provided as he works on a task, larger reinforcer provided upon completion of a task<br>• Verbal praise for work completion and other desired behaviors | • Frequent sensory/play breaks throughout the work session (e.g., 3 minutes of work, 3-minute break)<br>• Breaks include structured sensory activities (e.g., deep pressure, heavy work) and free-choice segments<br>• Weighted lap pad used as needed while working<br>• Water bottle with a resistant straw to drink from while working | • Specific language and social skills targets:<br>– Indicate preference and answer yes/no questions<br>– independently initiate a greeting when he comes to the work table<br>– Identify when help is needed and use a picture, sign, or verbal approximation to request help | • Create easy-to-use data sheets for each target skills<br>• Collect data on amount of time S attends to work | |

Many of these skills corresponded to several activities during the school day. For example, skills such as greetings, turn taking, and waiting were embedded in literacy and gross-motor groups. The team decided that these were so important that they would provide intense, systematic instruction for each of these skills during Sam's one-on-one sessions. Figures 11.9 and 11.10 depict the two classroom areas designed for individual instruction. Once Sam mastered a skill in the one-on-one sessions, they planned for generalization to the group activities. Generalization strategies included prompting the skills during each group activity and then gradually fading the amount of support provided.

In addition to systematically teaching the target skills, the team provided intense visual, sensory, and reinforcement supports. Visual/structural supports included the use a visual timer, token board, visual directions, and video models (see Figures 11.11 and 11.12). During the literacy groups, the team began by showing Sam a token board with five tokens. On the end of the board was a picture of the sensory area. After each of his turns, he removed a token from the board. When he had completed five turns, Sam was allowed to take a break in the sensory area.

The teacher supplemented her verbal directions with visual directions. When indicating to Sam that it was time to take his turn, for example, she held up an orange card with a picture indicating "your turn." Once Sam completed his turn, she handed him a picture card indicating "Wait."

The team also created video models to teach Sam the identified target skills. The video model was especially helpful in teaching appropriate use of playground equipment. The teacher videotaped two students playing appropriately on the jungle gym and the swings. Sam viewed the video each day before going to recess.

**Figure 11.9.** Area designed for individual work.

**Figure 11.10.** Area designed for individual work.

**Figure 11.11.** Sample visual support.

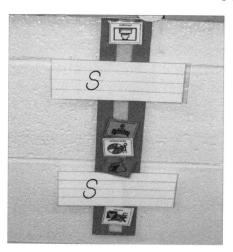

**Figure 11.12. Structure used for Sam's materials.**

Sensory supports also played an important part in increasing Sam's success at school. Instead of taking Sam to the track, the team worked to embed a variety of sensory activities throughout the school day. During group activities, he had access to items, such as water bottles with resistant straws, weighted lap pads, and chewy candy. During breaks, Sam engaged in a variety of activities, including carrying a weighted backpack, swinging, and lying under heavy blankets. The team reinforced Sam's choice-making skills by allowing him to choose his own sensory activities several times during the school day. Figure 11.13 depicts Sam's sensory area.

**Figure 11.13. Sensory area.**

The team realized that verbal praise alone was not reinforcing enough to promote learning and work completion for Sam. After talking with his mother, the teacher identified a variety of tangible reinforcers, such as small candy items, hot chocolate, and visually stimulating toys. Sam was also highly motivated to work for sensory breaks. As a result, the team embedded all of these items throughout the school day.

In addition to the sensory break, the teacher gave Sam a small piece of chewy candy after he completed each of his turns. She also used tangible reinforcers when Sam sat appropriately while others took their turns. Each tangible reinforcer was paired with verbal praise that clearly indicated the desired behavior. For example, when Sam sat and waited as a peer took a turn, the teacher handed him the piece of candy saying, "I like the way you are waiting quietly in your chair." Pairing the verbal praise with tangible reinforcers and sensory breaks proved highly motivating for Sam.

In addition to the visual/structural supports, the team used a variety of specific teaching strategies. The basis of these teaching strategies was systematic instruction and data collection. When teaching Sam to independently wait in a chair, for example, the team began by standing next to Sam as he sat in a chair for 15 seconds. At the end of the 15 seconds, the teacher provided reinforcement and directed Sam to the next task. They gradually increased the amount of time he waited in the chair and the distance between him and the teacher.

Data collection involved a variety of task analyses, checklists, and anecdotal records. The teacher created a data collection schedule that allowed her to take a great deal of data without feeling overwhelmed. She collected data on each academic skill at least once a week and data on Sam's behavior on a daily basis. These records supported the team in making decisions about the effectiveness of specific interventions and strategies and regarding Sam's behavior during the school day.

The interventions helped increase Sam's success during the school day, at home, and in the community. At the end of the school year, Sam will transition to a new teacher in a new school. This year he developed skills to support continual growth and a positive transition. Using CAPS, the new team will have insight into Sam's strengths and needs, and a solid base of interventions to start the school year.

# Home – Jason*

### By Jill Hudson, M.S.

Jason is a 12-year-old boy with ASD, who lives at home with mom and dad, two younger sisters, Stephanie and Michelle, and a dog and cat. He is in the sixth grade and participates in the general education classroom with modifications to the curriculum. He has been nonverbal since he was 3, but is showing some signs of functional verbal communication with the aid of PECS. Jason has difficulty discriminating letters and, therefore, has difficulty with words when reading sentences. He can match sight words to pictures when provided limited choices and can independently write his first name. In addition, Jason can sequence numbers up to 20 and use one-to-one correspondence up to 10. He responds well to physical and oral prompting. Jason has good navigation skills and is able to independently orient himself around the school. Each day, he delivers newspapers to specific rooms throughout the school.

Jason enjoys playing UNO, playing with beads, or drawing patterns on his whiteboard. These pastimes are frequently used as reinforcers at school. Transitions are the most difficult task for Jason. If a situation involves a new or unknown adult, he often becomes aggressive and throws items off his desk or kicks his chair to communicate what he cannot verbally express. To regulate himself, Jason often spins or talks in a loud voice. He is able to respond to redirection when given verbal or physical prompts.

193

*Thanks to Jason's father for developing this CAPS.

Jason enjoys being active, especially engaging in physical interactions with his peers and siblings. He typically exhibits a friendly, playful demeanor and has a sense of humor. He is comfortable participating in his community and is frequently found greeting people with whom he comes into contact.

Jason's typical routine at home after school includes down time and a quick snack before changing into more comfortable clothing. He prefers loose-fitting clothing that might not be appropriate for a school setting. There are continual attempts to communicate verbally with Jason during this time period. For example, asking, "What do you want to drink Jason?" and prompting him to respond by starting his sentence "I want _____". Approximately one half of the time he will answer with one word: *juice, soda,* or *drink*. If he is not given a drink, he independently goes to the refrigerator and gets what he wants. During an independent event like this, there is no communication or interaction with family members. Once a snack and drink are secured, Jason proceeds to the TV room to watch a favorite television show. If asked, "What do you want to watch, Jason?," he answers with *Sesame Street* or *Sponge Bob*. If he is not asked about a program, he uses the remote control to find it himself. During this time Jason may also independently go to his room to retrieve his beads or MP3 player. If he selects the MP3 player, he will bring it to a parent and pull on an arm or try to gain attention by saying "Mommy" or "Daddy" while handing his parent the player.

Jason joins the family for dinner and makes one-word requests for desired items. Afterwards, he helps clean up the dishes. Jason enjoys being near his family in the evening and initiates play interactions with his siblings. Occasionally, he prefers to be alone, but typically not for more than two hours. After some leisure time with his family, Jason begins his evening routine. This consists of completing any assigned schoolwork, taking a bath, reviewing his calendar, and going to bed.

## Strengths

Jason has many strengths, including his sense of humor. He often initiates playful behavior with his family members and enjoys wrestling and being tickled. He initiates verbal greetings with parents and siblings, including hugs. He can follow simple commands like "Put you dishes in the sink" or "Get your cup." He is friendly and comfortable and enjoys his time off from school by watching videos or listing to music, going into the community, and performing some life skills tasks.

## Needs

Jason needs to increase his verbalization skills and be able to ask for his needs, wants, and desires to be met. He currently grabs at things and people to initiate these things. Both parents agree that Jason's three biggest needs are (a) more verbalization, (b) more physical activity, and (c) increased social interaction with siblings.

# Comprehensive Autism Planning System

Jason's CAPS was designed by his father to be used for the home. Jason's father was attending a series of autism-related workshops where he learned about CAPS and thought this system would help Jason interact more with his family.  It builds in supports and structure for Jason as he enters an environment that should be relaxing, safe, and comfortable. By providing structure, in addition to the home being a place of respite, it provides opportunities to encourage skill development with his family and trusted community members. Jason's family did not opt to complete a baseline CAPS, instead they focused on creating the CAPS (see Figure 11.14).

## Figure 11.14. Home CAPS for Jason.

## Comprehensive Autism Planning System (CAPS)

Child/Student: __Jason__

| Activity | Targeted Skills to Teach | Structure/ Modifications | Reinforcement | Sensory Strategies | Social Skills/ Communication | Data Collection | Generalization |
|---|---|---|---|---|---|---|---|
| Home from school: • Greet family members • Have a quick snack and drink • Change clothing • Parents encourage Jason to talk about day at school by prompting | • Follows a daily schedule after coming home from school • Greets family members | • Visual schedule • Communication board | Hugs and greetings | • Hugs from family members • Greetings from all family members | • Smiles and laughs when he sees family members. • Hugs and says hi • Greets both sisters with hi and first names | Observation | • Communication board used throughout evening activities • Greeting in community |
| • Free time: • Watch TV • Listen to music on MP3 player • Play with beads • Play game with family | Parents encourage communication by oral prompting, "Do you want your music or beads" and "What show do you want to watch on TV?" | • Communication board • Scripts for playing games with family | Watching television programs and family interactions | Beads | Jason will respond to family members when asked what show he wants to watch on TV by saying either *Sesame Street* or *Sponge Bob* | Observation | Choicemaking at grocery store |
| • Dinner with family • Completes chore of putting away clean dishes and putting dirty dishes in dishwasher | Eat meal with family members | Communication board | Interaction is the reinforcer | Family members eat and encourage Jason to talk about meal | • Parents ask Jason what he wants for dinner • Family members eat and encourage Jason to talk about meal | Observation | • Ordering food at a restaurant and participating in conversation while there • Cleaning up room |

# Home CAPS for Jason (cont.)

| Activity | Targeted Skills to Teach | Structure/ Modifications | Reinforcement | Sensory Strategies | Social Skills/ Communication | Data Collection | Generalization |
|---|---|---|---|---|---|---|---|
| Complete assigned homework | ▪ Homework assignment completion<br>▪ Attending to task for 5 min. | Timer set for 5 minutes | Cutting and gluing activities | Working with different textures and products, like children's project glue | ▪ Parents go over homework with Jason with lots of encouragement, softly and slowly verbalizing to Jason; sometimes he requires hand-over-hand on written material<br>▪ Jason is interested in anything that involves making something; he likes cutting and working to glue paper symbols "pictures" in place | Observation | Independent work at school |
| Bedtime routine:<br>▪ Bath<br>▪ Calendar<br>▪ Prayers | Parents encourage communication by oral prompting, calendar routine, and scripted prayers | ▪ Calendar<br>▪ Scripted routine | Bath is reinforcing as is playing with beads in bed | Bath activities and beads | Jason remains close to family members during this time | Observation | Following routines on family outings |

Figure 11.15 provides a copy of Jason's social script that he can use to tell his sister and dad that he wants to exercise. Figure 11.16 shows the communication script that his sister uses to respond to Jason, and Figure 11.17 shows an example of Jason's communication board.

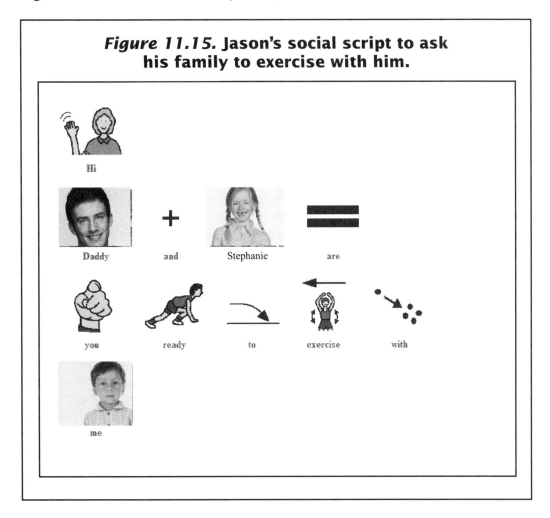

**Figure 11.15.** Jason's social script to ask his family to exercise with him.

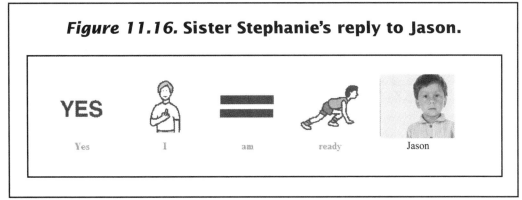

**Figure 11.16.** Sister Stephanie's reply to Jason.

*Figure 11.17.* **Sample communication board.**

# Middle/High School – Michael

*By Amy Bixler Coffin, M.S.*

Michael Thomas is a 16-year-old young man diagnosed with Asperger Syndrome (AS). He lives with his mother and two younger brothers, one of whom is diagnosed with attention deficit-hyperactivity disorder (ADHD) and obsessive compulsive disorder; the other has learning disabilities. Michael's mother and father divorced when Michael was 10 years old. Michael and his brothers spend every other Saturday with their father, who lives approximately 45 miles away. Mrs. Thomas is an LPN and works second shift from 3 to 11 p. m., four days a week. Her parents live in the same neighborhood as she and the boys and take turns caring for the boys while she is at work. Michael takes medication for anxiety as well as medication to assist with sleeping. Until recently, he had never slept through the night without waking up every two to three hours.

When Michael was approximately 3 years old, his mother noticed that he was developing differently from his same-age peers. He did not socialize and preferred to play alone. He would spend hours upon hours looking at books and magazines. He was very verbal in a "little professor-like" fashion. His expressive language skills far exceeded those of his peers. Michael showed signs of being very sensory defensive. Loud noises bothered him, as did being touched lightly. After a visit to his pediatrician, Michael's mother was assured that there was nothing wrong with her son and that she was overreacting. It was not until Michael turned 6 that he was diagnosed with AS.

Throughout elementary school Michael received special education services, including speech and language therapy focusing on pragmatic language and social skills and occupational therapy. After transitioning to middle school, Michael no longer received direct therapy services. At the end of eighth grade, he was dismissed from both therapies.

Michael is currently in the second quarter of his sophomore year of high school, attending all general education classes. He is enrolled in biology, history, English literature, algebra, composition, and physical education. His schedule also includes a daily support period where he is given assistance with organizational skills and social skills.

## Baseline CAPS

Due to a high number of discipline referrals and a decline in his grades, Michael's teachers decided to meet to complete a baseline CAPS. After discussing the requirements of each class, every teacher concluded that Michael was struggling in the following areas: completing independent work, working in groups, taking tests, participating in lectures appropriately, and completing homework assignments.

The staff then determined the specific skills that they believed to be the most important for him to learn, including task completion, attention to task, and conversational rules. Interventions currently being used were recorded; all of them were deemed appropriate to address targeted skills. Documentation of the various ways in which the team was collecting data was also recorded. Figure 11.18 shows Michael's baseline CAPS.

## Figure 11.18. Michael's baseline CAPS.

### BASELINE CAPS – Michael Thomas

| Activity | Targeted Skills to Teach | Structure/Modifications | Reinforcement | Sensory Strategies | Social Skills/ Communication | Data Collection | Generalization |
|---|---|---|---|---|---|---|---|
| **Independent Work** | Task completion | • School planner<br>• Verbal reminders by all teachers | • Completed in-class and homework assignments<br>• Good grades | | Asking for help when stuck | Teacher grade book | Hand in homework in other classes |
| **Group Work** | Conversational rules | • Teacher reminders with facial expressions of approval/ disapproval<br>• Assigned peer<br>• Weekly verbal reminders of group activities | Peer interaction | | Verbal reminders from teachers on what/how to interact in group after interaction occurs | Referrals to office or after-school detentions | |
| **Tests** | Task completion | • School planner<br>• Verbal reminders of upcoming tests<br>• Test dates announced by teachers | Test completion | | Asking for help when stuck | Test completion<br>Test scores | Use planner across classes |
| **Lectures** | Attention to task | • Sitting in front of room | Appropriate conversation | | Teacher cues on appropriate topics/ times to speak | Referrals to office or after-school detentions | |
| **Homework** | • Task completion<br>• Materials and supplies needed | • School planner<br>• Binder<br>• Book bag | • Homework turned in<br>• Higher grades on report card | | | Homework turned in complete | |

# Strengths

Michael is a very bright young man with an above-average IQ. He exhibits excellent rote memory skills, can quickly memorize the most recent statistics of any Major League baseball player, and can easily recall those stats when in conversation.

# Needs

Although he excels in math and history, he receives mostly C's on his report card due to the fact that 25% of grades for all academic classes is based on homework assignments. Michael has difficulty remembering to write his assignments down in his school planner and often forgets materials needed to complete assignments. As a result, he repeatedly does not do his homework and frequently does not remember to turn in assignments that he has completed.

Michael has very few friends at school. He tends to keep to himself in social situations. He prefers looking at sports magazines and memorizing baseball players' batting statistics rather than socializing with his peers when time allows. When he does participate in conversation with peers, he stands very close and often attempts to dominate the conversations around topics of his special interests, such as sports. When peers become uninterested in what he is saying, he does not recognize their nonverbal gestures or lack of interest. Although this interest is not atypical of peers his age, he has become obsessed with the topic and incessantly studies newspapers and books, often at inappropriate times during classes. Michael's mother reports that he does not have any friends that he associates with on the weekends or in the evenings. Instead, he prefers socializing with her and her friends.

# Michael's Comprehensive Autism Planning System (CAPS)

Michael's team began generating ideas for Michael's CAPS that would focus on strengthening existing skills, building new skills, and preventing challenging behaviors. The team members agreed that Michael needed supports to be presented visually as much as possible and, therefore, began modifying the interventions listed on his baseline CAPS, as most interventions were being presented orally. Figure 11.19 depicts Michael's M-CAPS and his traditional CAPS developed for his PE class.

One of the biggest areas of concern was that Michael learn to interact appropriately with peers and adults. To help develop this skill, visual supports were created, which included a hidden curriculum notebook and commenting cue cards. Sensory supports such as coping cards (see Figure 11.20) and a Stress Thermometer (see Figure 11.21) were also designed to assist Michael in self-monitoring his behavior when with peers and adults.

Taking into consideration Michael's special interests, the team crafted reinforcements to help motivate him to complete tasks and follow classroom rules. The reinforcer menu consisted of sports activities. Similarly, Michael's mother created a reinforcer menu for home to help encourage him to complete homework assignments (see Figure 11.22).

## Figure 11.19. Michael's M-CAPS.

### Modified Comprehensive Planning System (M-CAPS)
### Michael Thomas

| Activity | Targeted Skills to Teach | Structure/Modifications | Reinforcement | Sensory Strategies | Social Skills/ Communication | Data Collection | Generalization |
|---|---|---|---|---|---|---|---|
| **Independent Work** | Task completion | • Task organizer (prompt to use)<br>• Organization calendar (prompt to use)<br>• Systematic fading procedures for independent use<br>• Peer buddies | • Calming skills<br>• Appropriate conversation<br>• Completing homework/in-class work (from reinforcement menu) | • Relaxation techniques<br>• Coping cards<br>• Stress Thermometer | Asking for help when stuck | Task completion | Use task organizer and organization calendar across day |
| **Group Work** | Conversational rules | • Task organizer (prompt to use)<br>• Organization calendar (prompt to use)<br>• Systematic fading procedures for independent use<br>• Peer buddies | • Calming skills<br>• Appropriate conversation<br>• Completing homework/in-class work (from reinforcement menu) | • Relaxation techniques<br>• Coping cards<br>• Ear plugs<br>• Stress Thermometer<br>• Take a break card | • Conversation cues<br>• Comic Strip Conversations™<br>• Hidden curriculum notebook<br>• Cues for commenting and asking questions<br>• Social Stories™ | Appropriate comments during group (measured 1x per week) | Use hidden curriculum information during Scouts meetings |
| **Tests** | Task completion | • Task organizer (prompt to use)<br>• Orally administered tests | • Calming skills<br>• Appropriate conversation<br>• Test completion | • Fidget at desk<br>• Earplugs | Cues for commenting and asking question | Test grades | |
| **Lectures** | Attention to task | • Task organizer (prompt to use)<br>• Systematic fading procedures for independent use<br>• Lecture notes provided | • Calming skills<br>• Appropriate conversation | Fidget at desk | • Conversation cues<br>• Comic Strip Conversations™<br>• Hidden curriculum notebook<br>• Cues for commenting and asking questions | | |
| **Homework** | • Task completion<br>• Materials and supplies needed | Homework checklist (prompt to use and double check with student) | Homework turned in (reinforcement menu) | • Quiet area to complete<br>• Frequent breaks | NA | Homework turned in complete | |

## CAPS – Specific
## Physical Education Class – Michael Thomas

| Activity | Targeted Skills to Teach | Structure/Modifications | Reinforcement | Sensory Strategies | Social Skills/ Communication | Data Collection | Generalization |
|---|---|---|---|---|---|---|---|
| **PE** | ▪ Participation in group sports<br>▪ Accepting loss | ▪ Calendar of competitive sports<br>▪ Run errands, as needed (behavior: space invasion, loud voice; when game ends)<br>▪ Review sportsmanship guidelines (with entire class) using cue cards<br>▪ Present miniature cue card at 5-minute warning | ▪ Participation<br>▪ Accepting loss (use reinforcement menu)<br>▪ Social reinforcer | ▪ Ear plugs<br>▪ Calming cards<br>▪ Sensory breaks<br>▪ Stress Thermometer | ▪ Game statistician<br>▪ Peer buddy<br>▪ Social Story™ | ▪ Time in PE<br>▪ Number of meltdowns | Accept loss during games in Scouts |

**Figure 11.20.** Coping cards.

Take 2 deep breaths with
eyes closed.

Press hands together and
count to 10 slowly.

Repeat to myself 3 times
"Breathe in; hold;
breathe out."

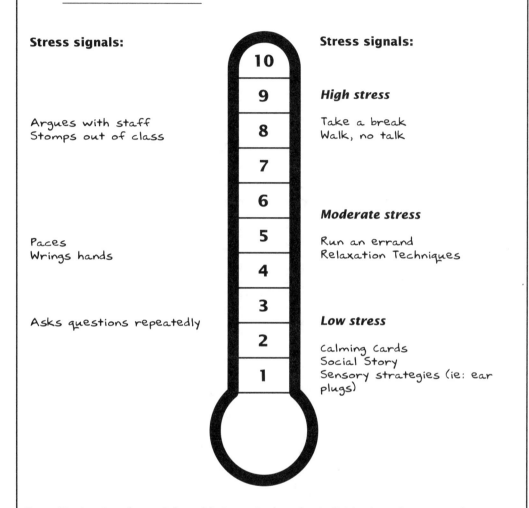

## Figure 11.21. Stress thermometer.
### PE Class

**For:** Michael Thomas

**Stress signals:**

Argues with staff
Stomps out of class

Paces
Wrings hands

Asks questions repeatedly

**10**
**9**
**8**
**7**
**6**
**5**
**4**
**3**
**2**
**1**

**Stress signals:**

*High stress*

Take a break
Walk, no talk

*Moderate stress*

Run an errand
Relaxation Techniques

*Low stress*

Calming Cards
Social Story
Sensory strategies (ie: ear plugs)

Case Studies

**Figure 11.22.** Reinforcer menus for school and home.

### School Reinforcer Menu for Michael

| MY REWARDS |
| --- |
| ▪ 10 minutes of reviewing baseball statistics in personal magazines/books |
| ▪ 15 minutes to do research on the Internet on baseball/ sports statistics/events |
| ▪ Time to browse books in the school library |

### Home Reinforcer Menu for Michael

| MY REWARDS |
| --- |
| ▪ 30 minutes of time to browse the web |
| ▪ Trip to local baseball cards store |
| ▪ 30 minutes of video games |

Recognizing that Michael struggles with organizational skills, supports were put into place to provide him with the structure necessary to organize himself and his school materials. These included activity calendars, including one for a long-term writing assignment (see Figure 11.23).

## Figure 11.23. Activity calendar.

### Composition: Writing Assignment

| Sunday | Monday | Tuesday | Wednesday | Thursday | Friday | Saturday |
|--------|--------|---------|-----------|----------|--------|----------|
| | | | 1 | 2<br>Have topic chosen for composition | 3 | 4 |
| 5 | 6 | 7 | 8<br>Have outline completed for composition | 9<br>Begin research for composition | 10<br>Continue research | 11 |
| 12 | 13<br>Continue research | 14<br>Continue research | 15<br>Continue research | 16<br>Continue research | 17<br>Continue research | 18 |
| 19 | 20<br>Turn in graphic organizer for composition | 21<br>Begin writing rough draft | 22<br>Continue writing rough draft | 23<br>Continue writing rough draft | 24<br>Continue writing rough draft | 25 |
| 26 | 27<br>Continue writing rough draft | 28<br>Finish writing rough draft | 29<br>Turn in first rough draft of composition | 30 | | |

Michael's PE class was modified to address his sensory needs. Supports, such as ear plugs, were provided to assist him in participating in group sports activities. Visual supports, including a calendar of competitive sports (see Figure 11.24), were developed to provide him with more structure.

Michael's teachers met approximately once a month for the remainder of the school year to revisit his CAPS, giving them the opportunity to review data collected on the various supports being used. Minor adjustments were made to his CAPS, as needed.

# Summary

As illustrated in the case studies in this chapter, CAPS, including Baseline CAPS and M-Caps (Modified Comprehensive Autism Planning System), is adaptable across ages, settings, educational levels, and activities. As such, it is an invaluable tool for helping teams, as well as parents, tie all the pieces together to structure and implement a successful program for students with ASD. Finally, due to its comprehensive nature, CAPS addresses current educational mandates and trends, including No Child Left Behind, response to intervention, and positive behavior supports.

## *Figure 11.24.* Calendar of competitive sports.

### Team Sports Calendar (PE, 4th quarter)

| Sunday | Monday | Tuesday | Wednesday | Thursday | Friday | Saturday |
|---|---|---|---|---|---|---|
| | | | 1 | 2 | 3 | 4 |
| 5 | 6<br>Team sports softball | 7<br>Team sports softball | 8<br>Team sports softball | 9 | 10 | 11 |
| 12 | 13 | 14 | 15<br>Team sports softball | 16<br>Team sports softball | 17<br>Team sports softball | 18 |
| 19 | 20 | 21 | 22 | 23<br>Team sports volleyball | 24<br>Team sports volleyball | 25 |
| 26 | 27<br>Team sports volleyball | 28<br>Team sports volleyball | | | | |

# APPENDIX

# Comprehensive Autism Planning System (CAPS)

Child/Student: _____

| Time | Activity | Targeted Skills to Teach | Structure/ Modifications | Reinforcement | Sensory Strategies | Communication/ Social Skills | Data Collection | Generalization Plan |
|------|----------|--------------------------|--------------------------|---------------|--------------------|------------------------------|-----------------|---------------------|
|      |          |                          |                          |               |                    |                              |                 |                     |
|      |          |                          |                          |               |                    |                              |                 |                     |
|      |          |                          |                          |               |                    |                              |                 |                     |
|      |          |                          |                          |               |                    |                              |                 |                     |
|      |          |                          |                          |               |                    |                              |                 |                     |
|      |          |                          |                          |               |                    |                              |                 |                     |

*ss=state standard

From Henry, S. A., & Myles, B. S. (2007). *The Comprehensive Autism Planning System (CAPS) for Individuals with Asperger Syndrome, Autism, and Related Disabilities*. Shawnee Mission, KS: Autism Asperger Publishing Company. www.asperger.net; used with permission.

# Modified Comprehensive Autism Planning Systems (M-CAPS)

Child/Student: _____

| Activity | Targeted Skills to Teach | Structure/ Modifications | Reinforcement | Sensory Strategies | Social Skills/ Communication | Data Collection | Generalization |
|---|---|---|---|---|---|---|---|
| **Independent Work** | | | | | | | |
| **Group Work** | | | | | | | |
| **Tests** | | | | | | | |
| **Lectures** | | | | | | | |
| **Homework** | | | | | | | |

From Henry, S. A., & Myles, B. S. (2007). *The Comprehensive Autism Planning System (CAPS) for Individuals with Asperger Syndrome, Autism, and Related Disabilities*. Shawnee Mission, KS: Autism Asperger Publishing Company. www.asperger.net; used with permission.

## Generalized Use of Supports

| CAPS Categories | Support | Is Used During ... | May Also Be Used ... |
|---|---|---|---|
| | | | |
| | | | |
| | | | |
| | | | |
| | | | |

# CAPS Support Development Form

| Support | Who Will Develop Support | Date Support Needed | Who Will Teach Support Use | When to Evaluate Effectiveness | How to Evaluate Effectiveness |
|---------|--------------------------|---------------------|----------------------------|--------------------------------|-------------------------------|
|         |                          |                     |                            |                                |                               |
|         |                          |                     |                            |                                |                               |
|         |                          |                     |                            |                                |                               |
|         |                          |                     |                            |                                |                               |
|         |                          |                     |                            |                                |                               |

# INDEX

# APC

Autism Asperger Publishing Co.
P.O. Box 23173
Shawnee Mission, Kansas 66283-0173
www.asperger.net